Set Another Place...
Company's Coming!

Written by
Bobbie R. Adams

Elise, May your home always be blessed with good food, family and friends

Bobbie R. Adams
4-22-06

Art Designs by Mary Knape
Chandler, Arizona
(KnapeArt@aol.com)

Photos from Nova Development

By Bobbie R. Adams

Additional copies may be obtained at the cost of $19.95,
plus $3.50 postage and handling, each book.
Texas residents add 8.25% sales tax, each book.

Send to:

Bobbie R. Adams

1911 Spring Hollow Path

Round Rock, Texas

78681-4052

Copyright © 2002

Round Rock, Texas

First Printing,   November 2002

ISBN: 0-9723641-0-2

WIMMER
COOKBOOKS
ConsolidatedGraphics
1-800-548-2537

Introduction

When I decided to write this cookbook and started thinking of a title to put on the cover, I settled on, *"Set Another Place, Company's Coming"*, because it reflects the open and friendly attitude of my family and of many other families when I was growing up. Extra family members and friends were always welcome at out dinner table and they didn't go away hungry. Sharing a meal with other people was simply the friendly thing to do in our family.

I grew up in rural Texas in the years following World War II. Indeed as a small child, I can remember the long line of troop transport vehicles carrying soldiers through Buffalo, Texas to points unknown. My folks were a farm family who always had a large garden filled with vegetables of every description. Canning fresh vegetables each spring and summer was a necessity and just a part of life. Baking bread and biscuits was as natural to my mother, Sally White, as any other household activity.

My mother taught me the art of cooking from a very early age. She was an excellent cook and was still turning out her favorite cakes and pies into her late 80's. By the time I was eleven or twelve, I was trying recipes on my own, sometimes with success and sometimes not, but always with the helpful encouragement of my mother. Indeed, I began collecting recipes as a teenager and still have several of them in my fifty plus year old collection.

In high school, I became active in the Future Homemakers of America (FHA), but it was my high school home economics teacher, Mrs. Ruth Tomme that had a great influence on me during those informative years. Her great dedication and encouragement is one reason why I sought and obtained a degree in Home Economics from the University of Texas and then became a hospital dietitian and later a teacher of Science and Home Economics.

Be my guest and enjoy the wonderful recipes I have collected, used, and perfected over the past fifty plus years. Cooking and entertaining can be fun and very rewarding. You don't have to be a great cook, but it does help if you enjoy cooking.

This book has plenty of delicious everyday recipes. Many are quick and easy while others take more time to prepare. Most of the ingredients you need are readily available and may already be on your pantry shelves.

Why not invite some friends over, set a few more plates at the table, cook up some fabulous dishes, and enjoy great fellowship and food! "Company's Coming." Bon appetit.

Bobbie R. Adams

Acknowledgement

My friend, Mary Knape has done a terrific job developing the cover design and dividers for this cookbook. Her expertise and knowledge has been invaluable.

My husband, George C. Adams has been the backbone of this effort. Without his help and encouragement this book would not have been possible. He spent countless hours assisting me with research, proof reading, and working on the computer.

Thanks to all my friends who have shared recipes with me over the years. A number of these tried and true favorites are included in this book. A special thanks to Pauline Maxwell who shared her special recipes for this book.

Table of Contents

Appetizers
&
Beverages

Appetizers & Beverages

Appetizers

Beverages

Sweet and Spicy Pecan Halves

2	cups pecan halves	½	teaspoon chili powder
2	tablespoons margarine, melted	¼	teaspoon dried crushed red pepper
1	tablespoon sugar		
½	teaspoon ground cumin	⅛	teaspoon salt

Preheat oven to 325 degrees. In a medium bowl, toss the pecans with the margarine; set aside. Combine the remaining ingredients in a small bowl; stir to blend. Sprinkle the seasonings over the pecans and toss to coat. Spread pecans on a large baking sheet; bake for about 15 minutes, stirring occasionally. Cool and store in airtight container.

Yield: 2 cups

Chunky Guacamole Dip

3	medium-size ripe avocados	2	tablespoons fresh lime juice
¼	cup finely chopped white onion	¼	teaspoon salt
1	medium-size ripe tomato, finely chopped		Dash hot pepper sauce (optional)

Peel avocados and remove pits. In a medium bowl, mash avocados with a fork until blended, but still chunky. Stir in the onion, tomato, lime juice, and salt. Stir to blend. If desired, add a dash of hot pepper sauce. Spoon into serving dish; place plastic wrap directly on the surface to keep it from browning too quickly. Refrigerate until ready to serve.

Yield: 2 cups

Note: It's not true that burying the avocado pit in the guacamole helps maintain good color. Adding fresh lemon or lime juice helps, however, it's best to prepare avocados just before serving. To ripen avocados, place in a paper bag and set aside at room temperature for 2 to 4 days then store in the refrigerator.

Spicy Shrimp Dip

1   (8 ounce) package cream
    cheese, softened
½   cup sour cream
½   cup picante sauce, any variety

½   bunch green onions, chopped
    (white and green parts)
½   pound cooked shrimp, peeled,
    deveined, diced
    Assorted crackers

In a medium bowl, mix the cream cheese and sour cream until well blended. Stir in the picante sauce and green onions; stir to blend. Add shrimp and stir gently to evenly distribute ingredients. Spoon into serving dish; cover with plastic wrap and refrigerate until ready to serve. Serve dip with assorted crackers.

Yield: 3½ cups

Olive Cheese Ball

1   (8 ounce) package cream cheese
1   (4 ounce) package blue cheese
1½ sticks margarine, softened
1   tablespoon lemon juice
2   tablespoons finely chopped
    onion

1   cup ripe olives, chopped,
    drained
2   tablespoons minced fresh
    parsley
½   cup finely chopped pecans

In a medium bowl, mix the cream cheese, blue cheese, and margarine together until well blended. Add the lemon juice, onion, and olives; stir to blend; set aside. Toss together the parsley and pecans. Shape cheese into a ball and roll in parsley and pecan mixture. Wrap in plastic wrap and refrigerate until ready to serve.

Yield: 3½ cups

Note: There are more than thirty varieties of parsley, but only two varieties are currently popular. The curly-leaf is most often used as a garnish since it does not wilt as quickly. The stronger flavored flat-leaf or Italian parsley is usually used for cooking.

Onion-Pecan-Cheese Mold

1 (16 ounce) package sharp Cheddar cheese, grated
2 cups mayonnaise
1 onion, finely chopped
1 clove garlic, pressed

Hot pepper sauce (4 to 5 drops)
1 cup finely chopped pecans
1 (8 ounce) jar strawberry jam
Shredded wheat and round buttery crackers

In a large bowl, combine the Cheddar cheese and mayonnaise; stir to blend. Add the onion, garlic, hot pepper sauce, and pecans; mix all ingredients thoroughly. Press into a 6 cup lightly greased ring mold. Chill. Remove from mold onto serving dish. Serve with a dish of strawberry jam in the center of mold and crackers surrounding mold.

Yield: 5½ cups

Walnut and Blue Cheese Spread

3 (8 ounce) packages cream cheese, softened
1 (4 ounce) package blue cheese, crumbled
1 stick margarine, softened

¾ cup chopped walnuts, toasted, divided
¾ cup chopped fresh chives, divided
1 (16 ounce) round bread loaf

In a large bowl, combine cheeses and margarine; stir to blend. Add ½ cup walnuts and ½ cup chives; blend all ingredients thoroughly. Cover and chill mixture 8 hours or overnight. Let stand at room temperature to soften. Hollow out bread loaf, leaving a 1-inch-thick shell. Spoon softened cheese spread into shell. Garnish with the remaining walnuts and chives. Cut bread removed from the inside of loaf into 1 inch cubes; serve with spread.

Yield: 5 cups

Note: This spread is also good served with fruits such as crisp apple or pear slices. Vegetables such as celery, carrots, or cucumbers are also excellent when served with this spread.

Baked Green Chilies and Cheese Dish

1 (8 ounce) package Cheddar cheese, grated
1 (8 ounce) package Monterey Jack cheese, grated
1 (4½ ounce) can chopped green chilies
Margarine

2 eggs, separated
⅓ cup condensed milk
1½ teaspoons all-purpose flour
¼ teaspoon salt
⅛ teaspoon pepper

Preheat oven to 325 degrees. In a medium bowl, combine cheeses; add green chilies and mix lightly to blend. Heavily grease an 8 inch square baking dish with margarine; spoon cheese mixture into dish. Separate the eggs; set yolks aside. Beat whites until just stiff and set aside. In a small bowl combine egg yolks and remaining four ingredients; whisk to blend thoroughly. Fold egg whites into egg yolk mixture. Pour egg mixture on top of cheese. With a fork, ooze egg mixture gently into cheese so that part of the egg mixture drains down into the cheese. Bake 45 to 60 minutes, or until knife inserted comes out clean. Cheese will begin to brown slightly on top. Cool in pan for a few minutes; cut into 1 inch squares and serve.

Yield: 64 servings

Sausage-Cheese Cocktail Balls

1 (1 pound) package hot bulk pork sausage
1 (8 ounce) jar processed cheese sauce

3 cups buttermilk biscuit baking mix

Preheat oven to 300 degrees. Combine sausage, cheese sauce, and biscuit mix in a large bowl; stir mixture until completely blended. Shape mixture into cocktail-size meatballs and place on a large ungreased baking sheet. Bake for 25 minutes or until lightly browned.

Yield: 4 dozen balls

Salmon Cheese Ball

1	(8 ounce) package cream cheese, softened	½	teaspoon garlic powder
1	cup grated Cheddar cheese	1	tablespoon lemon juice
2	tablespoons minced onion	1	teaspoon liquid smoke
1	tablespoon dried parsley flakes	1	(7.5 ounce) can pink salmon
¾	teaspoon celery salt	½	cup chopped pecans
			Assorted crackers

In a large bowl, mix together the cheeses. Add onion and the next 5 ingredients; stir until well blended. Remove any bones from salmon and flake; add to cheese mixture and mix thoroughly. Shape into a ball and roll in pecans. Chill for several hours. Serve salmon ball on a serving dish surrounded with assorted crackers.

Yield: 3 cups

Baked Cheese-Artichoke Dip

1	(14 ounce) can artichoke hearts	1	tablespoon fresh lemon juice
1	cup mayonnaise		Round buttery crackers
1	cup Parmesan cheese		

Preheat oven to 350 degrees. Drain artichoke hearts thoroughly and chop; place in a medium bowl. Add mayonnaise, Parmesan cheese, and lemon juice; stir to blend. Spread mixture into a lightly greased 8 inch square baking dish. Bake for about 30 minutes or until bubbly. Serve hot with buttery crackers.

Yield: 3½ cups

Spinach and Artichoke Dip

¾	cup minced onion	½	cup Parmesan cheese
2	tablespoons minced garlic	1	(6 ounce) jar artichoke hearts, drained, chopped
2	tablespoons olive oil		
1	cup heavy cream	1	(10 ounce) package frozen spinach, drained, chopped
1	cup finely grated Monterey Jack cheese		Salt and freshly ground pepper

In a medium saucepan, sauté onion and garlic in olive oil until tender. Add cream and simmer for about 3 minutes. Stir in the Monterey Jack and Parmesan cheese; simmer for 1 minute until cheese melts. Add artichokes and spinach; simmer for about 2 minutes to heat mixture. Season with salt and pepper. Spoon mixture into a 1½ quart serving dish; serve warm.

Yield: 5 cups

Note: Monterey Jack Cheese is a semi-soft cheese with a buttery ivory color and a mild flavor. The unaged variety is typically ripened for about one week. Its high moisture content and good melting properties makes it excellent for cooked dishes such as this recipe.

Texas Crock Pot Dip

1	pound lean ground beef	1	(10 ounce) can tomatoes and green chilies
1	pound pork sausage		
1	(1 pound) package processed cheese loaf	2	(10¾ ounce) cans cream of mushroom soup, undiluted
			Tortilla chips

In a large skillet, cook ground beef and sausage over medium-high heat, until meat is no longer pink; drain well. While meat is cooking, cut cheese into cubes and put into crock pot to melt. Combine cooked meat, tomatoes and green chilies, and mushroom soup with the cheese; stir to blend. Set temperature control on low and heat thoroughly. Serve dip with tortilla chips.

Yield: 8 cups dip

Creamy Tomato-Cheese Dip
with Herbs

1   (7 ounce) jar sun-dried tomato halves packed in oil, drained
2   tablespoons fresh lemon juice
2   cloves garlic, minced
2   tablespoons, minced fresh parsley
2   tablespoons, minced fresh basil
1   (8 ounce) package cream cheese, softened
1   cup sour cream
    Salt and pepper
    French bread, thinly sliced

Thoroughly drain the tomato halves and pat dry; place into a food processor with the lemon juice, garlic, parsley, and basil. Process ingredients until smooth. Add the cream cheese and sour cream; continue processing until all ingredients are well blended and smooth. Season with salt and pepper. Spoon mixture into a 1 quart serving dish; serve with French bread.

Yield: 3 cups

Note: The original sun dried tomatoes from Italy were left out in the sun to dry, then packed in olive oil. The "sun-dried" tomatoes we find today are usually dried in a dehydrator and then oil packed. These tomatoes have a chewy texture and sweeter flavor.

Marinated Mushrooms

1   pound fresh white mushrooms
2   tablespoons fresh lemon juice
2   quarts boiling water
1   (8 ounce) bottle Italian dressing
1/8 teaspoon garlic powder

Clean mushrooms by wiping with a damp paper towel or rinsing with cold water. Combine the lemon juice with the boiling water; add mushrooms. Cover; remove saucepan from burner and allow mushrooms to set for 5 minutes. Drain mushrooms and place into a quart jar or bowl. Pour Italian dressing over mushrooms and add garlic powder; stir and refrigerate for 24 hours before serving.

Yield: 8 to 10 servings

All-Time Favorite Spinach Dip

1   (10 ounce) package frozen
    chopped spinach
1   cup mayonnaise
1   cup sour cream
1   (2 ounce) package vegetable
    soup mix

⅛   teaspoon garlic powder
½   cup finely chopped onion
1   (8 ounce) can water chestnuts,
    drained, chopped
    Round loaf of French bread

Thaw spinach and drain thoroughly; pat dry with paper towels; set aside. In a medium bowl, combine the mayonnaise, sour cream, vegetable soup mix, and garlic powder; whisk together to blend. Add the onion, water chestnuts, and spinach; blend thoroughly. Refrigerate until ready to serve. Slice off the top of the bread and pull out the center to make a bowl. Spoon the dip into the bread bowl. Cut bread from the center into 1 inch cubes and serve with dip.

Yield: 4 cups dip

Note: Water chestnuts are the edible tubers of a water plant indigenous to Southeast Asia. They are slightly sweet, crunchy, and juicy. Water chestnuts add a nice texture to this dip as well as to many casserole dishes.

Baked Zucchini Squares

½   cup buttermilk biscuit baking
    mix
½   cup Parmesan cheese
½   teaspoon dried oregano
2   eggs, well beaten

1   stick margarine, melted
1½ cups zucchini (2 medium,
    unpeeled, sliced)
½   cup chopped onions

Preheat oven to 350 degrees. In a medium bowl, combine the baking mix, Parmesan cheese, and oregano; stir to blend. Add the eggs and margarine; stir only enough to blend. Fold in the zucchini and onions; stir to combine. Pour mixture into a greased 8 inch square baking dish or quiche dish; bake for 30 to 45 minutes or until lightly browned on top. Cut into squares or wedges and serve hot.

Yield: 12 squares or 8 wedges

Stuffed Mushroom Appetizers

½	pound fresh white mushrooms	½	teaspoon salt
¼	cup finely chopped shallots	⅛	teaspoon cayenne
4	tablespoons (½ stick) margarine	1	teaspoon lemon juice
2	tablespoons all-purpose flour	2	tablespoons Parmesan cheese
1	cup heavy cream		

Preheat oven to 350 degrees. Clean mushrooms by wiping with a damp paper towel. Remove stems and chop fine; reserve caps. In a medium skillet, sauté shallots in margarine over medium heat about 4 minutes. Add chopped mushroom stems and continue cooking for about 10 minutes or until moisture is evaporated. Remove from heat; sprinkle flour over mushrooms and stir to blend. Add cream and return to heat. Cook until mixture thickens. Add salt, cayenne, and lemon juice; stir to blend. Set mixture aside to cool. If mushrooms are being served later; refrigerate mixture until ready to use. Fill mushrooms, heaping slightly. Sprinkle with Parmesan cheese. Bake 10 minutes.

Yield: 15 to 20 appetizers

Note: If shallots are unavailable, substitute 2 tablespoons finely chopped onion. Shallots are preferable since their flavor is more delicate and they dissolve easily in liquid. Shallots are a separate member of the onion family and are not baby onions.

Urban Cowboy Layered Tex-Mex Dip

1 (16 ounce) can refried fat free beans
2 cups sour cream
1 (1¼ ounce) package taco seasoning mix
1 (8 ounce) jar picante sauce
4 ripe avocados, mashed
2 teaspoons lemon juice

2 medium tomatoes, chopped
1 bunch green onions, thinly sliced (white and green parts)
1 (8 ounce) package Cheddar cheese, grated
1 (4 ounce) can ripe olives, drained, chopped
Tostados

Spread refried beans on bottom of a shallow 2 quart salad bowl or a nacho baker. Mix sour cream and taco seasoning; spread on top of bean layer. Layer picante sauce. Mash avocados and mix with lemon juice; spread on top of picante sauce. Continue layering the remaining ingredients in order listed, except the tostados. Cover dip and refrigerate until ready to serve. Serve with tostados.

Yield: 12 or more servings

Miniature Cream Puffs
with Chicken Filling

Cream Puffs

6	tablespoons (¾ stick) margarine	¾	cup sifted all-purpose flour
¾	cup water	3	eggs

Chicken Filling

1	(12 ounce) can chicken, chopped fine	1	tablespoon dry onion salad dressing mix
1	cup finely chopped celery	2	tablespoons fresh lemon juice
½	cup mayonnaise		

Preheat oven to 425 degrees. In a small saucepan, combine the margarine and water; bring to a boil. Reduce heat; add flour all at one time, stirring rapidly. Cook and stir until mixture thickens and leaves side of pan. Remove from heat; add eggs, one at a time, beating well after each addition. Beat until mixture looks satiny and breaks off when spoon is raised. Drop from teaspoon onto ungreased baking sheet. Bake for 20 to 30 minutes or until browned. Let cool. To prepare filling, place chicken in a medium mixing bowl. Add remaining ingredients and mix well. Slice tops from cooled cream puffs and fill with chicken filling.

Yield: 4½ dozen cream puffs

Note: The pastry used to make these miniature cream puffs can also be used to make larger cream puffs, eclairs, and other pastries. Fill large pastries with whipped cream, custard, or other fillings.

Hye Roller Sandwiches

½ (16 ounce) can whole cranberry sauce

2 (8 ounce) containers whipped cream cheese

1 (1 pound) package lavosh bread (4 sheets)

2 heads green leaf lettuce, washed, thoroughly dried

5 large tomatoes, thinly sliced, drained on paper towels

1½ pounds thinly sliced turkey breast (deli-style)

1 pound thinly sliced Swiss cheese

In a medium bowl, mix the cranberry sauce and cream cheese. Spread thin on lavosh bread. Cover with lettuce, leaving 1 inch at edges without fillings. Place a row of tomato slices down the middle of bread lengthwise and two slices across. Place a single layer of turkey about 5 inches wide down the middle; repeat with the cheese. Roll up tightly lengthwise, but not so tight that the lavosh breaks. Cut each roll in half for easier handling. Wrap in plastic wrap. Place on a large tray and refrigerate overnight. To serve, slice sandwiches into 1½ inch widths. Serve on platter lined with lettuce leaves.

Yield: approximately 40 slices

Note: Lavosh bread is a round, thin, crisp bread that's also known as Armenian cracker bread. It comes in various sizes and is available in Middle Eastern markets.

Spring Cooler

1 (12 ounce) can frozen orange juice concentrate, undiluted

2 (12 ounce) cans frozen apple juice concentrate, undiluted

2 (1 quart) bottles club soda, chilled

Place orange juice and apple juice concentrates into a 1 gallon container; allow to thaw slightly. Add club soda and gently stir. Serve mixture in large glasses with crushed ice.

Yield: 12 (8 ounce) servings

Special Summer Fruit Punch

1	cup fresh mint leaves, loosely packed	3	cups orange juice
2	cups hot water	1	pint fresh strawberries, quartered
2½	cups sugar	2	(46 ounce) cans pineapple juice, chilled
2	cups cold water		
1½	cups fresh lemon juice	2	(1 quart) bottles ginger ale, chilled
½	cup fresh lime juice		

Place the mint leaves in a small bowl; add the hot water; let stand for 30 minutes. Pour mint water through a wire-mesh strainer into a 1 gallon container; discard mint leaves. Add the sugar and next 4 ingredients; chill for several hours. Pour mixture into a large punch bowl over crushed ice. Add strawberries, pineapple juice, and ginger ale. Serve.

Yield: 7 quarts

Citrus Punch

1	(46 ounce) can pineapple juice	¼	cup fresh lime juice
1½	cups orange juice	1¼	cups sugar
¾	cup fresh lemon juice	2	(1 quart) bottles ginger ale, chilled

Pour the pineapple juice into a 1 gallon container; add all remaining ingredients except the ginger ale and stir until sugar dissolves. Pour mixture into ice cube trays; freeze until firm. Place 4 to 6 cubes into each tall glass. Pour ginger ale over cubes; stir gently and let set until mixture becomes slushy. Serve.

Yield: 10 (12 ounce) servings

Note: You may freeze this citrus punch in an airtight container for later use. Thaw slightly and place in a punch bowl; add the ginger ale and stir until slushy, then serve.

Strawberry-Lemonade Punch

2   (12 ounce) cans frozen pink
    lemonade concentrate,
    undiluted
1   (12 ounce) can frozen orange
    juice concentrate, undiluted

2   (10 ounce) packages frozen
    sliced strawberries
6   cups water
1   (64 ounce) bottle ginger ale,
    chilled

Combine lemonade, orange juice, strawberries, and water in a 1 gallon container; stir to blend. Refrigerate juices until ready to serve. Pour lemonade mixture into a large punch bowl over crushed ice; add ginger ale slowly. Serve.

Yield: 21 servings (8 ounces each)

Note: If serving punch in a glass punch bowl, always temper the bowl before adding ice or cold liquids. Glass contracts and expands slightly with temperature changes. If a change takes place too quickly, the container will break. The same is true when washing the bowl. Slowly warm the bowl with water before washing.

Wedding Punch

1   (6 ounce) can frozen lemonade
    concentrate, undiluted
2   cups water
1   (24 ounce) bottle white grape
    juice, chilled

1   (32 ounce) bottle apple juice,
    chilled
1   (1 quart) bottle ginger ale,
    chilled
1   pint whole strawberries,
    washed

Combine the frozen lemonade and water in a 1 gallon container; stir to dissolve lemonade. Add the grape and apple juice. Refrigerate until ready to serve. Pour mixture into a large punch bowl over crushed ice. Slowly pour in ginger ale; add strawberries. Serve.

Yield: 3 quarts

Pineapple-Lime Punch

2 cups sugar
2 (.13 ounce) packages unsweetened lime-flavored drink mix powder

2 quarts water
1 (46 ounce) can pineapple juice
1 quart ginger ale

Place sugar and lime-flavored drink mix into a 1 gallon container; add water and stir until sugar and drink mix dissolves. Add pineapple juice; refrigerate until ready to serve. Pour mixture into a large punch bowl over crushed ice; add ginger ale and serve.

Yield: 5 quarts

Frozen Banana Punch

4 cups sugar
6 cups water
6 bananas
1 (46 ounce) can pineapple juice, divided

2 (12 ounce) cans frozen orange juice concentrate, undiluted
1 (12 ounce) can frozen lemonade concentrate, undiluted
6 (1 quart) bottles lemon-lime soda

In a medium saucepan, combine the sugar and water. Bring to boiling, stirring until sugar is dissolved; remove from heat and cool. In a blender, combine the bananas and a small amount of the pineapple juice; blend until smooth. Pour the banana mixture into a large container. Stir in the cooled syrup, the remaining pineapple juice, orange juice, and lemonade. Stir to mix well. Pour fruit mixture into 3 large containers that will hold 3 or more quarts each (clean, empty milk cartons work well here) and freeze. To serve, remove from freezer 2 hours before serving to allow mixture to soften. Place mixture into a punch bowl and add ginger ale slowly. Stir gently to combine.

Yield: 48 (8 ounce) servings

Cranberry-Citrus Punch

1½ cups sugar	1 (6 ounce) can frozen orange juice concentrate, undiluted
1½ cups water	
1 (32 ounce) bottle cranberry juice cocktail	1 (46 ounce) can unsweetened pineapple juice
1 (12 ounce) can frozen lemonade concentrate, undiluted	5½ cups water
	1 (32 ounce) bottle ginger ale

Place sugar and 1½ cups water into a medium saucepan. Bring to a boil; heat until sugar dissolves; set aside to cool. Combine sugar syrup and the next 5 ingredients in a 1½ gallon container. Refrigerate until ready to serve. In a large punch bowl pour juice mixture over crushed ice; slowly pour in ginger ale. Serve.

Yield: 24 (8 ounce) servings

Hot Spiced Tea

1 gallon water	2 cups sugar
1 teaspoon whole cloves	Juice of 2 lemons, plus rind of 1
3 sticks cinnamon, broken	⅔ cup fresh orange juice
1 (1 ounce) tea bag	½ cup grapefruit juice

In a large container, bring water to boiling. Tie cloves and cinnamon together in a cloth bag; add spice and tea bag to water; steep. Remove tea and spice bag; add sugar to warm tea mixture and stir to dissolve. Add lemon juice, lemon rind, orange juice, and grapefruit juice. Simmer over very low heat. Strain and serve hot.

Yield: 5 quarts spiced tea

Note: This recipe is from my college days. During finals, our dorm mother always had this tea available whenever we needed a break from studying. The tea was served from a tea pot she brought back from China where she and her husband once served as missionaries.

Christmas Wassail

2	quarts apple cider	1	stick cinnamon
2	cups orange juice	1	teaspoon whole cloves
1	cup lemon juice	½	cup (packed) light brown sugar
1	(46 ounce) can pineapple juice		

Combine all ingredients in a stock pot that is 1½ gallons or larger. Simmer until flavors are blended. Strain and serve hot.

Yield: 17 (8 ounce) servings

Note: This recipe can also be prepared in a large coffee server and served directly from the pot. Traditionally, wassail was served in a large bowl, garnished with small roasted apples and ladled into servings cups.

Hot Spiced Cranberry Punch

1	(32 ounce) bottle cranberry juice cocktail	⅔	cup (packed) dark brown sugar
5	cups pineapple juice	4	sticks cinnamon, broken
1	cup water	1	tablespoon whole cloves
		1	teaspoon whole allspice

Pour cranberry juice, pineapple juice, and water into a 12 cup percolator. Stir in brown sugar. Place cinnamon, cloves, and allspice into basket; perk as for coffee.

Yield: 10 (8 ounce) servings

Note: This recipe can be doubled and prepared in a large 30 cup coffee server. If coffee container is not available, simmer the ingredients in a large stock pot on top of the stove.

Instant Russian Tea

1	cup powdered orange drink mix	½	teaspoon ground cloves
½	cup instant tea	½	teaspoon ground allspice
1	cup sugar	1	(.13 ounce) package
1	teaspoon ground cinnamon		unsweetened lemonade mix

Combine all the ingredients together in a small bowl; mix well. Store in a tightly sealed container. To serve, stir 2 to 3 teaspoonfuls (more or less if preferred) into 1 cup boiling water.

Yield: approximately 2½ cups mix

Mexican Hot Chocolate

¼	cup unsweetened cocoa powder	¾	teaspoon vanilla extract
¼	cup sugar		Whipped cream (optional)
¾	teaspoon ground cinnamon		Chocolate sprinkles (optional)
4	cups milk, divided	4	sticks cinnamon (optional)
¼	cup half-and-half		

In a small bowl, mix cocoa powder, sugar, and cinnamon. In a medium sauce-pan, heat 1 cup milk; stir in cocoa mixture and whisk until smooth. Reduce heat to low and heat until almost boiling, stirring constantly. Whisk in remaining 3 cups milk, cream, and vanilla extract. Heat to almost boiling. Remove from heat and whisk until frothy. Pour into cups. If desired, top with whipped cream, chocolate sprinkles, and serve with stick cinnamon.

Yield: 4 servings

Chocolate-Cinnamon Coffee

¼	cup coffee grounds	1	stick cinnamon, broken
¼	teaspoon hot chocolate mix	8	cups water

Place coffee grounds into a coffee filter; sprinkle hot chocolate mix and cinnamon on top of the coffee. Add water to coffee maker and brew.

Yield: 8 cups

Breads & Brunch

Breads & Brunch

Breads

Brunch

Southern-Style Buttermilk Corn Bread

2	cups yellow cornmeal	2½	cups buttermilk	
1	cup all-purpose flour	2	eggs	
2	teaspoons baking soda	4	tablespoons (½ stick) margarine	
1	teaspoon salt			

Preheat oven to 450 degrees. Sift cornmeal, flour, soda, and salt together into a large bowl; set aside. Whisk buttermilk and eggs together in a small bowl and add to dry ingredients; stir just enough to blend. Heat margarine in a heavy 9 inch skillet, allowing skillet to be completely greased. Pour excess margarine into corn bread mix; blend. Pour batter into hot skillet and bake for about 20 minutes or until browned.

Yield: 12 servings or 6 cups crumbs for dressing

Note: This all-American favorite is usually made with yellow or white cornmeal. I prefer yellow cornmeal. This corn bread is best when baked in an iron skillet. I recommend the skillet or baking pan be hot when the batter is added. This allows the bread to bake quicker and produces a moist light corn bread.

Corn Bread Delight

2	eggs, beaten	1	onion, chopped
1	cup sour cream	2	(8½ ounce) boxes corn bread mix
1	(8¾ ounce) can whole kernel corn, drained	1	stick margarine
1	(8½ ounce) can cream-style corn		

Preheat oven to 450 degrees. In a large bowl combine eggs, sour cream, corn, and onion. Add corn bread mix and stir to blend. Melt the margarine in a 13 x 9 inch pan, allowing pan to be completely greased. Pour excess margarine into corn bread mixture and stir to blend. Spoon batter into the hot baking pan and bake for 35 to 40 minutes.

Yield: 12 servings

Tex-Mex Corn Bread

¾   cup yellow cornmeal
¼   cup all-purpose flour
½   teaspoon salt
½   teaspoon baking powder
¼   teaspoon baking soda
1   tablespoon sugar
1   egg
1   cup buttermilk
½   medium onion, chopped

½   medium bell pepper, chopped
     (or 2-3 jalapeño peppers
     chopped fine)
1   (8¾ ounce) can whole kernel
     corn, drained
¾   cup (3 ounces) grated Cheddar
     cheese
¼   cup bacon drippings

Preheat oven to 450 degrees. Sift together the cornmeal and the next 5 ingredients into a large bowl. Set aside. Whisk together the egg and buttermilk; stir into dry ingredients. Add the onion, bell pepper or jalapeño peppers, corn, and cheese; stir to blend. Heat bacon drippings in a heavy 9 inch skillet, allowing skillet to be completely greased. Pour excess drippings into corn bread mixture; blend. Pour batter into hot skillet and bake for 20 to 25 minutes or until browned.

Yield: 12 servings

Broccoli Corn Bread

2   (8½ ounce) boxes corn bread
     mix
1   teaspoon salt
4   eggs, beaten
1   cup cottage cheese

1   large onion, chopped fine
1   (10 ounce) package frozen
     chopped broccoli, cooked
1   stick margarine

Preheat oven to 400 degrees. Put the corn bread mix into a large bowl; add salt and set aside. In a small bowl, combine eggs, cottage cheese, and onion. Drain broccoli and add to egg and cheese mixture; stir into corn bread mix. Melt the margarine in a 13 x 9 inch baking pan, allowing pan to be completely greased. Pour excess margarine into corn bread mixture and stir to blend. Spoon batter into baking pan; bake for 30 to 40 minutes.

Yield: 12 servings

Buttered Corn Sticks

4	tablespoons (½ stick) margarine	¼	teaspoon garlic powder	
1	tablespoon Parmesan cheese	2	cups buttermilk biscuit baking mix	
½	teaspoon dried basil leaves			
¼	teaspoon dried oregano leaves	1	(8¾ ounce) can cream-style corn	

Preheat oven to 450 degrees. Melt margarine in a small covered dish in the microwave oven; add Parmesan cheese, basil, oregano, and garlic powder. Mix and set aside. In a medium bowl, combine the baking mix and corn; stir until soft dough is formed. Knead dough several times on a floured surface. Roll dough into a rectangle about ½ inch thick. Cut into 1 x 3 inch strips. Roll strips in seasoned margarine. Bake on a 15 x 10 inch baking pan for 10 to 12 minutes or until lightly browned.

Yield: approximate 20 small corn sticks

Note: This is a tasty and interesting way to prepare corn sticks. You can experiment with the seasoning by making additions or substitutions as you prefer.

Old South Hushpuppies

2	cups white cornmeal	3½	cups boiling water
1	teaspoon salt	4	tablespoons (½ stick) margarine
1	teaspoon baking powder		Cooking oil or shortening
3	tablespoons sugar		

In a small bowl, sift together cornmeal, salt, baking powder, and sugar. Add slowly to water, stirring briskly. When smooth, remove from heat and stir in margarine; cool. Form into round finger-size strips. Fry in 2 inches of cooking oil or shortening until browned. Drain on paper towels. Serve hot.

Yield: 30 to 40 hushpuppies

Note: As you may have heard, there is a great story behind the name "hush-puppies." Hunters would supposedly fry these corn sticks from left over corn-meal, then throw them to their hunting dogs who were whining for food, while saying: "hush puppies." Makes a great story anyway!

Southern Corn Muffins with Ham

2	eggs, beaten	1	cup yellow cornmeal
1½	cups buttermilk	1	cup all-purpose flour
1	stick margarine, melted	1½	tablespoons sugar
1	(8¾ ounce) can whole kernel corn, drained	2	teaspoons baking powder
		1	teaspoon baking soda
½	cup shredded ham	½	teaspoon salt

Preheat oven to 450 degrees. In a small bowl, whisk together the eggs, butter-milk, and margarine; add the corn and ham; set aside. In a large bowl, sift together the cornmeal and the remaining 5 ingredients. Pour ham and corn mixture into the dry ingredients and stir only until the ingredients are blended. Grease 12 medium-size muffin tins and place into oven for about 10 minutes to heat. Remove from oven and fill cups two-thirds full. Bake for about 15 to 20 minutes.

Yield: 12 servings

Buttermilk Biscuits

2 cups all-purpose flour	4 tablespoons solid vegetable shortening
½ teaspoon salt	
¼ teaspoon baking soda	¾ cups buttermilk
2 teaspoons baking powder	

Preheat oven to 450 degrees. In a medium bowl, sift together the flour, salt, baking soda, and baking powder. Using a pastry blender, cut shortening into dry ingredients. Add buttermilk and stir only until ingredients are moistened. Place dough onto a lightly floured board or wax paper and knead about 6 times. Roll to desired thickness and cut with biscuit cutter. Place biscuits on a lightly greased 11 x 7 inch baking sheet or iron skillet. Bake for 12 to 15 minutes.

Yield: 10 to 12 biscuits

Note: The secret to great biscuits is to work the dough only enough to distribute the leavening for even rising. My family always had biscuits for breakfast. Mother knew just how much to handle the dough and could make great biscuits in just minutes.

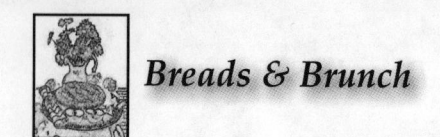

Sour Dough Biscuits

1 (¼ ounce) envelope active dry yeast	1 teaspoon baking soda
2 tablespoons warm water	1 teaspoon salt
5 cups all-purpose flour	1 cup solid vegetable shortening
3 tablespoons sugar	2 cups buttermilk
1 tablespoon baking powder	Margarine, melted

Preheat oven to 450 degrees. In a small bowl, dissolve the yeast in warm water; set aside. In a large bowl, sift together the flour, and the next 4 ingredients. Cut the shortening into the flour mixture. Stir the buttermilk into the yeast mixture; add to the dry ingredients and stir to mix. Turn dough onto a well floured board and knead enough to hold together. Roll dough to about ½ inch thickness and cut with biscuit cutter. Place biscuits on a greased 17 x 11 inch baking sheet and brush tops with margarine. Bake for 20 minutes or until golden browned.

Yield: 3 dozen biscuits

Note: This dough will keep refrigerated for several days. Allow the biscuits from refrigerated dough to rise about 15 minutes after cutting them out. This is also a great recipe for party biscuits.

Classic Cream Scones

2	cups all-purpose flour	1	egg
2	teaspoons baking powder	1½	teaspoons vanilla extract
⅛	teaspoon salt	1	egg white
¼	cup sugar	1	teaspoon water
5½	tablespoons margarine		Sugar
½	cup heavy cream		

Preheat oven to 425 degrees. In a large bowl, sift together the flour, baking powder, salt, and sugar. Cut in the margarine with a pastry blender until mixture is crumbly. Whisk together cream, egg, and vanilla extract; add to flour mixture; stirring just until dry ingredients are moistened. Turn dough out onto a lightly floured surface and knead gently just until dough holds together. Lightly roll the dough into a 10 inch circle that is 1 inch thick. Cut into wedges. Whisk together egg white and water; brush mixture over tops of scones. Sprinkle scones with additional sugar. Place on a lightly greased 11 x 7 inch baking sheet. Bake 18 to 20 minutes or until lightly browned.

Yield: 12 servings

Note: The original scones from Scotland were made with oats and griddle-baked. This modern version is made with flour and is slightly sweet. You can vary the recipe by adding different dried fruits and spices.

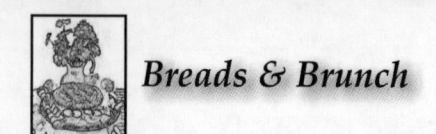

Herbed Yorkshire Puddings

3	eggs	1	tablespoon chopped fresh chives
1	cup whole milk		
1	cup all-purpose flour	2	teaspoons chopped fresh sage
¼	teaspoon salt	2	teaspoons chopped fresh thyme
1	tablespoon chopped fresh parsley	1	teaspoon chopped fresh rosemary
		4	tablespoons olive oil, divided

Preheat oven to 450 degrees. Whisk eggs and milk together in a medium bowl to blend. Sift flour and salt into egg mixture and blend. Add all of the herbs and whisk until well blended. Let batter stand at room temperature at least 30 minute or refrigerate up to 3 hours. Whisk before using. Place a standard 12 cup metal muffin pan into the oven and heat 10 minutes. Place 1 teaspoon olive oil into each muffin cup. Return pan to oven until oil is very hot. Immediately spoon 2 generous tablespoonfuls of batter into each muffin cup. Bake until puddings are golden and puffy, about 12 minutes. Puddings will sink in center but edges will stay puffy. Serve hot.

Yield: 12 servings

Whole-Wheat Popovers

⅓ cup all-purpose flour
⅔ cup whole-wheat flour
¼ teaspoon salt
⅞ cup (¾ cup, plus 2 tablespoons) milk

1 egg, beaten
1 teaspoon margarine, melted
4 tablespoons vegetable oil, divided

Preheat oven to 450 degrees. Sift the flour and salt into a small bowl; set aside. Whisk the milk and egg together; add margarine. Add liquid to the dry ingredients and beat vigorously until well blended. Place 1 teaspoon vegetable oil into each cup of a standard 12 cup muffin pan. Place into oven and heat about 10 minutes or until oil is very hot. Spoon batter evenly between muffin cups. Bake 30 to 35 minutes.

Yield: 12 servings

Note: This recipe originally appeared in a 1931 issue of the Better Homes and Gardens magazine. Times have changed, but good recipes have a lasting quality.

Southern-Style Muffins
with Orange Butter

Muffins

2	cups all-purpose flour	1	teaspoon salt
½	cup sugar	1	stick margarine, softened
1	tablespoon baking powder	¾	cup milk

Orange Butter

5½	tablespoons butter, softened	2½	cups powdered sugar
¼	cup frozen orange juice concentrate		

Preheat oven to 350 degrees. Sift the flour, sugar, baking powder and salt together into a medium bowl. Cut the margarine into the flour mixture with a pastry blender until it resembles coarse cornmeal. Add the milk to the flour mixture, stirring until just mixed. Drop spoonfuls of muffin mixture into 12 medium-size greased muffin tins. Tins should be about two-thirds full. Bake for 10 to 12 minutes or until just browned. Cream butter until light and fluffy. Add remaining ingredients and blend thoroughly. Serve butter with muffins. Refrigerate any left-over butter.

Yield: 12 muffins

Raisin Bubble Buns

2	cups sifted all-purpose flour	1	egg, beaten
¼	cup sugar	½	cup milk
3	teaspoons baking powder	4	tablespoons (½ stick) margarine
1	teaspoon salt	½	cup sugar
⅓	cup solid vegetable shortening	1	teaspoon ground cinnamon
⅔	cup seedless raisins	½	teaspoon ground nutmeg

Preheat oven to 400 degrees. Sift flour, sugar, baking powder, and salt together into a large mixing bowl. Cut in shortening until particles are size of small peas; add raisins and mix lightly. Whisk egg and milk together and combine with dry mixture, stirring until blended. Turn out onto lightly flour board and turn dough over several times to flour surface lightly. Divide dough into 4 equal parts. Shape each into a slender roll about 15 inches long. Melt margarine and set aside. Combine sugar, cinnamon, and nutmeg and stir to blend. Cut dough into ½ inch pieces and shape into balls. Dip each ball lightly in margarine; roll in mixture of sugar, cinnamon, and nutmeg. Pile 4 small balls into each greased medium-size muffin cup. Bake about 15 minutes or until crusty and golden browned. Serve hot.

Yield: 24 muffins

Sausage Biscuit Bites

¾ pound (hot or mild) bulk pork
   sausage
2⅔ cups all-purpose flour
2 tablespoons sugar
1 teaspoon baking powder
½ teaspoon baking soda
½ teaspoon salt

½ cup solid vegetable shortening
1 (¼ ounce) package active dry
   yeast
¼ cup warm water
1 cup buttermilk
   Margarine, melted

Preheat oven to 425 degrees. Cook sausage in a medium skillet until browned, stirring to crumble; drain well and set aside. Sift together into a large bowl the flour and the next 4 ingredients. Cut in the shortening until mixture resembles coarse meal. Add sausage and toss with dry ingredients. Dissolve yeast in water; let stand 5 minutes. Add yeast mixture to buttermilk and whisk to blend. Add buttermilk mixture to dry ingredients, stirring just until the dry ingredients are moistened. Turn dough out onto a lightly floured surface; knead lightly 3 to 4 times. Roll dough to ½ inch thickness; cut with a 1¾ inch round cutter. Place biscuits on an ungreased 15 x 10 inch baking sheet. Brush tops with margarine. Bake for 10 minutes or until golden browned.

Yield: 3 dozen biscuits

Refrigerator Potato Rolls

4	servings instant mashed potatoes	1	cup milk
4¾	cups all-purpose flour, divided	½	cup solid vegetable shortening
1	(¼ ounce) package active dry yeast	½	cup sugar
		1	teaspoon salt
		2	eggs, beaten

Preheat oven to 375 degrees. Prepare mashed potatoes according to package directions. In large mixer bowl, stir together 2 cups of the flour and the yeast. In a 1 quart saucepan, heat milk, shortening, sugar, and salt just until warm, stirring constantly to melt shortening; stir in potatoes. Add to dry mixture in mixer bowl; add eggs. Beat at low speed of electric mixer for about 1 minute, scraping sides of bowl constantly. Beat 3 minutes at high speed. By hand, stir in enough of the remaining flour to make a soft dough. Place dough into a greased bowl, turning once to grease surface. Cover; refrigerate several hours or up to a few days. To use, remove dough from refrigerator. Divide in half. Place ½ of the dough on a lightly floured board and divide into 12 equal pieces; form into smooth balls and place into a greased 9 inch square baking pan. Repeat with remaining dough. Cover and let rise until almost double, 45 to 60 minutes. Bake for 25 to 30 minutes or until browned. Serve hot.

Yield: 24 rolls

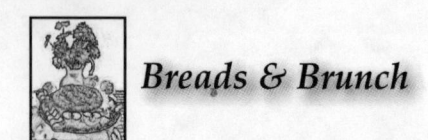

Gerri's Bran Dinner Rolls

2	(¼ ounce) envelopes active dry yeast	1	cup whole bran cereal
½	cup warm water	1	cup boiling water
¾	cup solid vegetable shortening	2	eggs, beaten
½	cup sugar	4½-5	cups all-purpose flour, divided
1	tablespoon salt		Margarine, melted

Preheat oven to 425 degrees. Dissolve yeast in water; set aside. In a large bowl combine shortening, sugar, salt, and whole bran cereal; pour the water over the ingredients and stir. Set aside to cool. Add eggs and yeast to the bran mixture. Beat in 2 cups flour. Add enough of the remaining flour to make a soft dough. Turn dough out onto a floured surface, knead until smooth and elastic. Place into a large, well greased bowl, turning to grease top. Cover bowl and let stand in a warm place, free from drafts, about 15 minutes. Divide dough into 2 portions and shape each portion into 12 balls; place into 2 greased (9 inch) square pans or greased muffin pans. Brush rolls with margarine. Cover and let rise 2 hours or until double in size. Bake 20 to 25 minutes. Serve hot.

Yield: 24 dinner rolls

Note: This dough can be refrigerated for later use. Do not knead dough before placing into the refrigerator.

Granola Bread with Cinnamon Butter

Cinnamon Butter

1   stick butter, softened

¼   teaspoon ground cinnamon

Granola Bread

6¼-6¾   cups unsifted all-purpose flour, divided

2   (¼ ounce) envelopes active dry yeast

1   tablespoon salt

1¼   cup water

1   cup milk

½   cup honey

¼   cup solid vegetable shortening

2   eggs, beaten

2   cups granola, crushed

Cream the butter until light and fluffy. Add cinnamon and blend thoroughly. Refrigerate until ready to serve. Preheat oven to 375 degrees. In a large mixing bowl combine 3 cups flour, yeast, and salt. In a 1 quart saucepan, heat the water, milk, honey, and shortening until the shortening melts. Add liquid to the flour and yeast mixture; add eggs. Beat on medium speed of mixer for 3 minutes. By hand stir in granola and enough flour to make a firm dough. Turn dough out onto a lightly floured board and knead until smooth and elastic. Place dough into a large greased bowl, turning to grease top. Cover and let rise until double in size; 1 to 2 hours. Divide dough in half. Roll each half into a 14 x 9 inch rectangle on a well floured board. Beginning with upper short side, roll dough toward you. Seal the dough into shape by pinching the center seam and ends. Fold sealed ends under. Place each loaf seam side down into a greased 9 x 5 inch loaf pan. Cover; let rise in warm place, free from draft, until double in bulk, about 1 hour. Bake for 30 to 35 minutes. Cover loosely with foil the last 5 to 10 minutes so bread does not become too brown on top. Serve plain or with cinnamon butter.

Yield: 2 loaves bread

Orange Rolls

Yeast Dough

1	(¼ ounce) envelope active dry yeast	1	egg, beaten
1	cup warm water	¾	teaspoon salt
3	tablespoons sugar	3-3½	cups all-purpose flour, divided
2	tablespoons solid vegetable shortening		

Filling

4	tablespoons (½ stick) margarine, softened	2	tablespoons sugar
		2	tablespoons grated orange rind

Topping

4	tablespoons (½ stick) margarine	1	tablespoon orange juice
¼	cup sour cream	6	tablespoons sugar

Preheat oven to 400 degrees. Place yeast and water into a large bowl; stir to dissolve. Add sugar, shortening, egg, salt, and 2 cups flour; beat on low speed of mixer until smooth. Stir in enough of the remaining flour to make a soft dough. Place dough into a greased bowl, turning to grease all sides. Cover and let rise in a warm place about 1 hour or until double in size. Punch dough down and turn out on a floured board. Knead dough several times. Roll into a rectangle. In a small bowl, combine the filling ingredients; spread filling on dough. Beginning with the upper short side, roll dough toward you. Pinch edges to seal. Cut into 1½ inch slices. Place rolls into a greased 13 x 9 inch pan. Cover, let rise in warm place until double in size. Bake 20 to 25 minutes or until lightly browned. Place the topping ingredients into a small saucepan; heat until all ingredients are blended. Pour topping over rolls when they are taken from the oven. Serve rolls hot or cold.

Yield: 18 rolls

Dill and Onion Casserole Bread

2-2⅔	cups all-purpose flour, divided	1	(¼ ounce) envelope active dry yeast
2	tablespoons sugar	¼	cup water
1	tablespoon instant minced onions	1	tablespoon margarine
		1	cup creamed cottage cheese
2	teaspoons dill seed	1	egg, beaten
1	teaspoon salt	2	tablespoons margarine, melted
¼	teaspoon baking soda	¼	teaspoon coarse salt (optional)

Preheat oven to 350 degrees. In a large bowl, combine 1 cup flour and next 6 ingredients; blend well. In a small saucepan, heat water, margarine, and cottage cheese until very warm. Add warm liquid and egg to the flour mixture. Using an electric mixer, blend at low speed until moistened; beat 3 minutes at medium speed. By hand, stir in remaining 1 to 1⅔ cups flour to form a stiff batter. Cover loosely with plastic wrap and cloth towel. Let rise in a warm place until double in size, about 1 hour. Stir dough down to remove all air bubbles. Place into a greased 1½ to 2 quart casserole. Cover, let rise in warm place until double in size about 30 to 45 minutes. Bake dough 30 to 40 minutes or until browned and loaf sounds hollow when lightly tapped. Remove from casserole dish; brush loaf with margarine; sprinkle with coarse salt, if desired. Cool on a wire rack. Slice and serve.

Yield: 1 (18-slice) loaf

Note: Batter breads are formed without kneading, however in order to stretch the gluten, they require vigorous beating. The dough should be stiff enough for a spoon to stand up in. The texture of batter breads will be less refined than kneaded breads.

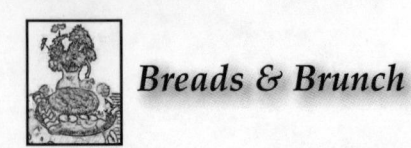

Savory Garlic Bread

1	stick margarine, softened	¼	teaspoon dill weed, crushed
1	teaspoon dried parsley flakes	1	clove garlic, finely minced
½	teaspoon dried oregano, crushed	1	large loaf French bread
			Parmesan cheese

Preheat oven to 400 degrees. In a small bowl, combine the margarine and the next 4 ingredients. Slice the bread into thick slices. Spread each slice generously with the herb mixture. Reassemble into loaf shape on a sheet of foil; wrap halfway up loaf, leaving top exposed. Spread remainder of herb mixture over the top and sprinkle generously with cheese. Heat bread for about 20 minutes or until hot.

Yield: 12 servings

Carrot Bread

2	cups all-purpose flour	½	cup flaked coconut
1½	cups sugar	½	cup chopped pecans
½	teaspoon salt	1	cup vegetable oil
2	teaspoons baking soda	3	eggs, beaten
2	teaspoons ground cinnamon	2	teaspoons vanilla extract
½	cup seedless raisins	2	cups grated raw carrots

Preheat oven to 350 degrees. Sift together into a large bowl the flour and the next 4 ingredients. Add the raisins, coconut, and pecans; toss with the dry ingredients. Add the vegetable oil, eggs, vanilla extract, and carrots; mix well. Spoon mixture into a well greased and floured 9 x 5 inch loaf pan; let stand 20 minutes. Bake 1 hour or until cake tester inserted into center comes out clean.

Yield: 1 large loaf

Banana Bread

2	sticks margarine	¼	teaspoon salt
3	cups sugar	½	cup buttermilk
2	teaspoons vanilla extract	2	cups (about 4 large) mashed ripe bananas
4	eggs	2	cups chopped pecans
3	cups all-purpose flour		
2	teaspoons baking soda		

Preheat oven to 350 degrees. In a large mixing bowl, cream margarine and sugar; add vanilla extract and eggs. Beat until light and fluffy. In a small bowl, sift together the flour, baking soda, and salt; add to creamed mixture. Add buttermilk and bananas and stir only until ingredients are mixed. Add pecans. Spoon mixture into a well greased and floured 9 x 5 inch baking pan and 6 muffin tins. Bake loaf for 1 hour and 15 minutes or until cake tester inserted into the center comes out clean. Bake muffins for about 30 minutes.

Yield: 1 loaf and 6 muffins

Note: This recipe makes a sweeter bread than some banana breads. It can also be baked in 2 smaller bread pans, if preferred. For the best results, always use really ripe bananas. Often the ripest bananas are those reduced for quick sale by supermarkets.

Zucchini Bread

1	cup vegetable oil	3	cups all-purpose flour
3	eggs, beaten	1	teaspoon baking soda
2	teaspoons vanilla extract	¼	teaspoon baking powder
2	cups sugar	1	teaspoon salt
2	cups grated raw zucchini, peeled	1	tablespoon ground cinnamon
		1	cup chopped pecans (optional)

Preheat oven to 325 degrees. Combine oil and the next 4 ingredients in a large bowl; blend well. Sift together the flour, and the next 4 ingredients; combine with zucchini mixture; stir just until mixture is thoroughly moistened. Stir in pecans. Pour batter into a well greased and floured 9 x 5 inch loaf pan lined with wax paper. Bake for about 1½ hours or until a cake tester inserted into the center comes out clean. Remove from pan and cool slightly; wrap in foil.

Yield: 1 large loaf

Note: This is an excellent recipe and easy to prepare. If using young, tender zucchini, omit peeling.

Tropical Bread

Bread

1½ cups all-purpose flour	½ cup chopped pecans
½ cup sugar	1 cup (about 2 large) mashed, ripe bananas
1 teaspoon baking powder	
1 teaspoon baking soda	1 (8 ounce) can crushed pineapple, undrained
½ teaspoon salt	
1 teaspoon ground cinnamon	¼ cup vegetable oil
1 cup quick cooking oats	2 eggs, beaten
½ cup flaked coconut	

Glaze

1 tablespoon margarine	½ teaspoon vanilla extract
1½ tablespoons milk	½ cup powdered sugar

Preheat oven to 350 degrees. In a large bowl, sift together the flour and the next 5 ingredients. Add oats, coconut, and pecans to dry mixture. In a medium bowl, mix bananas, pineapple, oil, and eggs; pour into dry ingredients. Stir just until liquid is absorbed and mixture is thoroughly moistened. Bake in a well greased and floured 9 x 5 inch loaf pan for 50 to 55 minutes or until cake tester inserted into center comes out clean. In a small saucepan heat the margarine, milk, and vanilla extract together. Stir in the powdered sugar and blend. Drizzle glaze over slightly cooled bread.

Yield: 1 large loaf

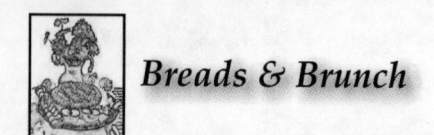

Bishop's Bread

1½ cups all-purpose flour, sifted	1 cup dates, finely chopped
1½ teaspoons baking powder	1 cup candied cherries, halved
¼ teaspoon salt	3 eggs, beaten
⅔ cup semi-sweet chocolate chips	1 cup sugar
2 cups walnuts, coarsely chopped	

Preheat oven to 325 degrees. Sift together into a large bowl the flour, baking powder, and salt. Add the chocolate chips, walnuts, dates, and candied cherries; stir until well coated. In a small bowl, combine eggs and sugar; beat thoroughly. Fold egg mixture into dry ingredients. Blend just until mixture is thoroughly moistened. Spoon mixture into a well greased and floured 9 x 5 inch loaf pan lined with wax paper. Bake for 1½ hours, or until a cake tester inserted into the center comes out clean. Remove from pan and cool slightly; wrap in foil.

Yield: l large loaf

Pumpkin Bread

2 cups all-purpose flour	4 eggs, beaten
2 cups sugar	1¼ cups vegetable oil
2 teaspoons baking soda	1 (15 ounce) can solid pack
1 teaspoon salt	pumpkin
1 tablespoon ground cinnamon	

Preheat oven to 350 degrees. Sift together into a medium bowl, the flour and the next 4 ingredients. In a large bowl, combine the eggs, oil, and pumpkin; beat 1 minute. Fold the dry ingredients into the liquid and beat on medium speed of mixer for 1 minute. Pour mixture into a well greased and floured 9 x 5 inch baking pan lined with wax paper. Bake for 1 hour or until cake tester inserted into center comes out clean. Cool for a few minutes in pan; remove from pan and wrap in foil.

Yield: 1 large loaf

Note: This is one of my favorite breads to serve during the fall season. It is delicious served plain or with soft cream cheese.

Date Loaf Bread

2	cups all-purpose flour, sifted	¾	cup solid vegetable shortening
1	teaspoon baking powder	1	cup (packed) light brown sugar
¼	teaspoon salt	2	eggs, beaten
1	(10 ounce) package pitted dates, chopped	1	teaspoon vanilla extract
		½	teaspoon baking soda
½	cup chopped walnuts	½	cup milk

Preheat oven to 350 degrees. Sift together into a medium bowl the flour, baking powder, and salt. Add dates and walnuts to the dry mixture. In a large bowl, cream the shortening and sugar until light and fluffy. Add eggs and vanilla extract; blend thoroughly. Dissolve the baking soda in the milk and add to the creamed mixture. Stir in dry ingredients and mix only until all ingredients are well blended. Pour mixture into a well greased and floured 9 x 5 inch pan that has been lined with wax paper. Bake for 50 to 60 minutes or until a cake tester inserted into the center comes out clean. Allow to cool in the pan a few minutes; remove loaf from pan and wrap in foil.

Yield: 1 large loaf

Raisin Spice Bread

1	cup quick cooking oats	½	teaspoon ground nutmeg
1	stick margarine	½	cup raisins
1	cup boiling water	1	cup pecans, chopped
1½	cup all-purpose flour	2	eggs, beaten
1	teaspoon baking soda	2	cups (packed) light brown sugar
½	teaspoon salt		
1	teaspoon ground cinnamon	1	teaspoon vanilla extract

Preheat oven to 350 degrees. In a large bowl, combine oats, margarine, and water; let set for 20 minutes. Sift together into a medium bowl the flour and the next 4 ingredients. Add raisins and pecans. Combine the eggs, sugar, and vanilla extract; stir into the oatmeal mixture and beat well. Pour the liquid mixture into the dry ingredients and stir only enough to blend. Spoon mixture into a well greased and floured 9 x 5 inch loaf pan that has been lined with wax paper. Bake for 1 hour and 15 minutes or until a cake tester inserted into the center comes out clean. Cool for a few minutes in pan; remove and wrap in foil.

Yield: 1 large loaf

Pistachio Banana Bread

2½	cups all-purpose flour	5	eggs, beaten
1½	cups sugar	1	teaspoon vanilla extract
½	teaspoon salt	1	cup vegetable oil
½	teaspoon baking soda	2	cups (about 4 large) mashed
2	(3.4 ounce) packages pistachio instant pudding		ripe bananas

Preheat oven to 350 degrees. In a large mixing bowl, sift together the flour, sugar, salt, and baking soda; stir in the pistachio pudding. In a medium bowl, combine eggs, vanilla extract, and oil; blend thoroughly. Add bananas to egg and oil mixture; stir to blend. Combine the liquid ingredients with dry ingredients. Stir only until ingredients are blended together. Spoon mixture into 2 well greased and floured 8 x 4 inch pans, lined with wax paper or a Bundt or tube pan. Bake 50 to 60 minutes for small pans; 1 hour and 15 minutes for large pan; or until a cake tester inserted into the center comes out clean. Cool a few minutes in pan and remove loaves and wrap in foil.

Yield: 2 small loaves or 1 large round loaf

Note: This bread can be served anytime of the year, but the light green color reminds me of Christmas. I usually double the recipe and bake three loaves in 9 x 5 inch pans to share with family and friends.

Strawberry Bread

4½	cups all-purpose flour	6	eggs, beaten
3	cups sugar	1½	cups vegetable oil
1½	teaspoons salt	2½	(10 ounce) packages frozen
1½	teaspoons baking soda		strawberries, thawed
1½	teaspoons ground cinnamon	1	teaspoon red food coloring

Preheat oven to 350 degrees. In a large bowl, sift together the flour and the next 4 ingredients. In another large bowl, combine the eggs and oil; add strawberries and red food coloring; continue beating until the strawberries are well blended. Make a well in center of the flour mixture and add liquid mixture. Stir only until the dry ingredients and liquid are blended. Grease and flour two (9 x 5 inch) loaf pans and line with wax paper. Divide batter between pans and bake for 1 hour and 15 minutes or until a cake tester inserted into the center comes out clean. Cool in pan for a few minutes; remove and wrap in foil.

Yield: 2 large loaves

Note: Quick bread loaves are done when the top is golden browned and a cake tester inserted into the center comes out clean. It is not unusual for a lengthwise crack to develop in the bread during the cooking process.

Oatmeal Muffins

1 cup quick cooking oats	1 egg
1 cup buttermilk	1 cup sifted all-purpose flour
5½ tablespoons margarine, softened	1 teaspoon baking powder
	½ teaspoon baking soda
½ cup (packed) light brown sugar	1 teaspoon salt

Preheat oven to 400 degrees. In a small bowl, soak together the oats and buttermilk for about 20 minutes. In a medium bowl, cream the margarine and sugar; add egg and beat until fluffy. Combine the oats and creamed mixture; stir to blend. In a small bowl, sift together the flour, baking powder, baking soda, and salt. Add the dry ingredients to the liquid mixture and stir only until blended. Fill 12 greased, medium-size muffins tins about two-thirds full. Bake for about 20 to 25 minutes. Remove form muffin tins and serve.

Yield: 12 muffins

Note: When preparing muffins, mix the dry ingredients and liquids only until the dry ingredients are moistened. A smooth batter will create tough, coarse-textured muffins with tunnels. I prefer to bake muffins in tins without paper or foil baking cups.

Cinnamon Muffins

Batter

5½ tablespoons margarine, softened	1½ teaspoons baking powder
½ cup sugar	½ teaspoon salt
1 egg, beaten	¼ teaspoon ground nutmeg
1½ cups sifted, all-purpose flour	½ cup milk

Topping

6 tablespoons (¾ stick) margarine, melted	½ cup sugar
	1 teaspoon ground cinnamon

Preheat oven to 350 degrees. In a medium bowl, cream the margarine and sugar; add egg and beat until fluffy. In a small bowl, sift together the flour, baking powder, salt, and nutmeg. Add the dry ingredients alternately with the milk, to the creamed mixture. Stir only until blended. Spoon batter into 12 well greased, medium-size muffin tins. Bake for 20 to 25 minutes. When baked remove immediately from muffin tins; roll in melted margarine and then in sugar and cinnamon. Serve hot.

Yield: 12 muffins

Country Bran Muffins

2 cups bran flakes	1 cup sifted, all-purpose flour
½ cup milk	2½ teaspoons baking powder
½ cup molasses	½ teaspoon salt
1 egg, beaten	½ cup seedless raisins
¼ cup solid vegetable shortening, melted	

Preheat oven to 400 degrees. In a medium bowl, combine bran flakes, milk, and molasses; let stand until most of the moisture is absorbed, about 20 minutes. Add egg and shortening; beat well. Sift together into a small bowl the flour, baking powder, and salt; stir in raisins and toss to blend. Add to the bran mixture; stir only until the liquid and dry ingredients are combined. Spoon batter into 12 well greased, medium-size muffin tins. Bake for about 20 minutes or until done.

Yield: 12 muffins

Blueberry Muffins

1 cup fresh or frozen blueberries	1 egg, beaten
1½ cups sifted, all-purpose flour	½ cup milk
2 teaspoons baking powder	2 tablespoons margarine, melted
½ teaspoon salt	Grated rind of 1 medium lemon
½ cup sugar	

Preheat oven to 400 degrees. If using fresh blueberries, wash and dry them thoroughly in a single layer on paper towels. If frozen blueberries are used, thaw completely and drain on paper towels. In a medium mixing bowl, sift together the flour, baking powder, salt and sugar. Add blueberries and toss to mix, being careful not to break the blueberries. In a small bowl, combine egg, milk, margarine, and lemon rind; whisk to blend ingredients. Add liquid ingredients to dry ingredients. Mix only until the dry ingredients are barely moistened. The batter will be slightly lumpy and quite thick. Spoon batter into 12 well greased, medium-size muffin tins; tins should be about two-thirds full. Bake 20 to 25 minutes or until golden browned. Serve immediately.

Yield: 12 muffins

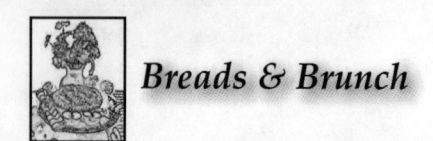

Pineapple Filled Sopaipillas

Sopaipillas

1¾ cup all-purpose flour
2   teaspoons baking powder
1   teaspoon salt

2   tablespoons solid vegetable shortening
⅔   cup cold water

Pineapple Filling

2½ tablespoons sugar
2   tablespoons cornstarch

1   (20 ounce) can crushed pineapple, undrained
Powdered sugar

In a small bowl, sift together the flour, baking powder, and salt. With a pastry blender, cut in shortening; add enough of the water to make a stiff dough. Turn dough onto a lightly floured board and knead lightly until smooth. Cover and let rise for 10 minutes. Roll dough to about ⅛ inch thickness; cut into 3-inch squares. Fry the squares in hot shortening; turn frequently so the sopaipillas will puff up evenly. Remove with slotted spoon and drain on paper towels. Serve with pineapple filling. To prepare the filling, blend the sugar and cornstarch together in a small saucepan; blend in the pineapple and cook until thickened. Fill each sopaipilla with 1 heaping tablespoonful of filling and roll in powdered sugar. Serve hot.

Yield: 18 to 20 sopaipillas

Note: Sopaipillas are often served with honey. The filling in this recipe provides another flavorful alternative.

Breakfast Casserole

1 pound pork sausage	6 eggs, beaten
10 white sandwich bread slices, cubed	2 cups milk
	1 teaspoon salt
2 cups (8 ounces) grated sharp Cheddar cheese	1 teaspoon dry mustard
	¼ teaspoon Worcestershire sauce

Preheat oven to 350 degrees. Cook sausage in a large skillet over medium heat, stirring until it crumbles and is no longer pink; drain well. Place bread cubes into a lightly greased 13 x 9 inch baking dish; sprinkle bread evenly with cheese, and top with sausage. Whisk eggs and the next 4 ingredients together; pour evenly over sausage mixture. Cover and chill casserole for 8 hours or overnight. Let stand at room temperature for 30 minutes before baking. Bake for 45 minutes or until set and lightly browned. Let stand 5 minutes before serving.

Yield: 6 to 8 servings

Note: Two cups cubed or shredded ham may be substituted for the sausage in this recipe. Deli ham is also very good as a substitute.

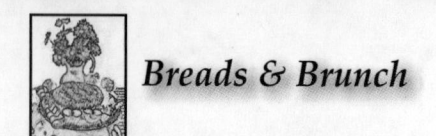

Mushroom and Onion Omelet

2	tablespoons margarine	6	eggs
6	large white mushrooms, sliced	1	tablespoon water
4	green onions, chopped and divided (white and green parts)	¼	teaspoon salt
		¼	teaspoon ground black pepper
		2	teaspoons margarine, divided

Melt 2 tablespoons margarine in a small skillet over medium-high heat. Add mushrooms and half of the onions; sauté 3 minutes. Set aside. Whisk eggs, water, salt, and pepper in a medium bowl to blend. Melt 1 teaspoon margarine in a small nonstick skillet over medium heat. Add half of egg mixture. Stir with back of fork until edges begin to set. Cook until omelet is set, lifting edges with spatula to let uncooked egg flow underneath, about 2 minutes. Spoon half of mushroom mixture down center of omelet. Fold both sides of omelet over filling and transfer to plate. Repeat with remaining margarine, egg mixture, and mushroom mixture. Sprinkle omelets with remaining onions and serve.

Yield: 2 servings

Note: This recipe can easily be doubled or tripled. Other ingredients that may be added are cheese, tomatoes, bell peppers, and chopped ripe black olives.

Scrambled Eggs Supreme

½	teaspoon chili powder	½	teaspoon Worcestershire sauce
⅛	teaspoon ground cumin	½	cup (2 ounces) grated Cheddar
⅛	teaspoon dried oregano		cheese
8	eggs	¼	teaspoon garlic salt
¼	cup cottage cheese	¼	teaspoon black pepper
⅓	cup buttermilk		Salt
½	teaspoon hot pepper sauce		

Combine the chili powder, cumin, and oregano in a small bowl and mix well to crush the oregano leaves. Break eggs into a separate bowl and whisk. Add the chili powder mixture, cottage cheese, and the next 6 ingredients; stir just until mixed. Season with salt. Pour mixture into a nonstick skillet. Cook until soft scrambled, stirring frequently. Serve immediately.

Yield: 4 servings

Quiche Lorraine

6	slices cooked ham	4	eggs
6	slices Swiss cheese	1	cup half-and-half
1	(9-inch) pastry crust, 1½ inches deep, pre-cooked		Salt and pepper
			Ground nutmeg

Preheat oven to 375 degree. Arrange slices of ham and cheese alternately in the pie crust. Whisk together the eggs and half-and-half; season with salt and pepper. Pour mixture into pie crust and sprinkle with nutmeg. Bake for about 45 minutes or until custard is set. Serve hot.

Yield: 8 servings

Note: To pre-cooked crust, place a piece of buttered aluminum foil on top. Cover foil with a layer of dried beans. Bake shell for 15 to 20 minutes in a preheated 425 degree oven. Remove foil and beans. With a pastry brush, coat entire shell with egg yolk and bake an additional 2 minutes.

Baked Vegetable Frittata

4	eggs, beaten
¾	cup mayonnaise
3	cups grated zucchini
2	cups grated carrots
¼	cup chopped onion
1	tablespoon chopped fresh basil

1½	cups all-purpose flour
1	cup (4 ounces) grated Cheddar cheese
½	cup Parmesan cheese
	Freshly ground black pepper

Preheat oven to 375 degrees. Whisk together the eggs and mayonnaise. Stir in the zucchini, carrots, onion, and basil. Toss the flour with the cheese and stir into the egg mixture. Season with pepper. Pour batter into a greased 10 x 2 inch quiche pan. Bake for 30 to 35 minutes or until set. Serve hot.

Yield: 6 to 8 servings

Note: A frittata is an Italian omelet. They are firmer than a French omelet and are generally cooked on the stove top. This one however is oven baked.

Texas Grits

3	cups water
1	teaspoon salt
¾	cup grits
6	tablespoons (¾ stick) margarine

½	pound processed cheese loaf, cubed
2	eggs, beaten
¼	teaspoon hot pepper sauce
	Paprika

Preheat oven to 250 degrees. Bring water to boiling in a 2 quart saucepan. Add salt and grits; simmer until the grits are cooked. Add the margarine and cheese; stir until cheese melts. Add eggs and pepper sauce. Pour ingredients into a lightly greased 9 inch square baking dish. Sprinkle with paprika. Bake for about 1 hour.

Yield: 6 servings

Note: This is an excellent brunch dish. Bake in a 13 x 9 inch dish if you double the recipe. To vary the recipe, add 1 pound cooked and crumbled sausage or ½ to 1 can of diced green chilies.

Breakfast Pudding Casserole

1 loaf cinnamon-raisin bread	1 tablespoon vanilla extract
5 eggs, beaten	1 teaspoon ground cinnamon
3 egg yolks	½ teaspoon ground nutmeg
¾ cup milk	1 stick margarine, melted
1 cup half-and-half	Powdered sugar

Preheat oven to 350 degrees. Grease two (9 inch) square baking pans; set aside. Trim crust from bread and cut into cubes. Place ½ of the bread cubes into each pan. Whisk together the eggs, and the next five ingredients; pour half of mixture into each pan. Cover and chill overnight. When ready to bake, drizzle margarine evenly over the casseroles. Bake for 45 to 60 minutes. Sprinkle with powdered sugar. Cut into squares and serve hot.

Yield: 12 servings

Basic Crêpes

3 eggs	4 tablespoons (½ stick)
1 cup milk	margarine, melted, divided
¼ teaspoon salt	Powdered sugar
½ cup all-purpose flour	

Whisk eggs, milk, and salt together in a medium bowl to blend. Add flour and whisk until smooth. Whisk in 2 tablespoons margarine. Heat a 5-inch-diameter skillet over medium heat. Brush with melted margarine. Pour 2 tablespoons batter into skillet and swirl to coat bottom. Cook until edge of crêpe is light browned, about 30 seconds. Loosen edges gently with spatula. Carefully turn crêpe over. Cook until crêpe is just cooked through, about 15 seconds. Transfer to plate and cover with paper towel. Repeat with remaining batter, brushing skillet with more melted margarine. Spoon any desired filling into center of crêpes and roll up. Dust with powdered sugar and serve.

Yield: 14 crêpes

Presidential Waffles

1	tablespoon sugar	4	teaspoons baking powder
1	stick margarine	¼	teaspoon salt
2	egg yolks	⅞	cup milk
1	cup all-purpose flour	2	egg whites, stiffly beaten

In a medium bowl, cream the sugar and margarine; add the egg yolks and beat until light and fluffy. Sift together into a small bowl the flour, baking powder, and salt; add flour mixture alternately with milk to the creamed mixture. Fold in the egg whites. Bake on a hot waffle iron. Serve with butter and maple syrup.

Yield: 2 servings

Note: This recipe was originally published in a small book of White House recipes in 1962. Supposedly, it was President Kennedy's breakfast treat on special occasions. The waffles are rich, crisp, and delicious. Sprinkle in chopped pecans for a variation.

Spicy Buttermilk Coffee Cake

2¼	cups all-purpose flour	¾	cup sugar
½	teaspoon salt	¾	cup vegetable oil
2	teaspoons ground cinnamon, divided	1	cup chopped pecans
¼	teaspoon ground ginger	1	teaspoon baking soda
1	cup (packed) light brown sugar	1	teaspoon baking powder
		1	egg, beaten
		1	cup buttermilk

Preheat oven to 350 degrees. Combine flour, salt, 1 teaspoon cinnamon, ginger, sugars, and vegetable oil. Remove ¾ cup mixture; add pecans and remaining cinnamon. Set aside for topping. To remaining batter, add soda, baking powder, egg, and buttermilk; stir to blend. Small lumps in the batter are fine. Pour batter into a well greased 13 x 9 inch pan. Sprinkle topping over the surface. Bake 40 to 50 minutes or until cake tester inserted into the center comes out clean.

Yield: 12 servings

Buttermilk Pancakes
with Honey-Pecan Butter

Honey Butter

1	stick butter, softened
1	cup pecan halves

¼ cup light clover honey

Pancakes

1 cup all-purpose flour
1 tablespoon sugar
½ teaspoon salt
1 teaspoon baking powder

½ teaspoon baking soda
1 egg, beaten
2 tablespoons vegetable oil
1 cup buttermilk

Combine butter, pecan halves, and honey in a food processor. Push on and off several times to blend; pecans should remain somewhat chunky. Pour into a small serving dish and set aside. In a medium bowl, sift together the flour and the next 4 ingredients. In another bowl, whisk the egg, oil, and buttermilk thoroughly to blend. Add the liquid ingredients to the dry ingredients and beat until smooth. Cook on a hot griddle. Serve hot with honey pecan butter.

Yield: 6 medium pancakes

Streusel Coffee Cake

Cake Batter

¾ cup sugar
4 tablespoons (½ stick) margarine
1 egg
½ teaspoon vanilla extract

1½ cups sifted all-purpose flour
2 teaspoons baking powder
½ teaspoon salt
½ cup milk

Topping

½ cup (packed) light brown sugar
2 tablespoons all-purpose flour
2 teaspoons ground cinnamon

2 tablespoons (¼ stick) margarine, melted
½ cup chopped pecans

Preheat oven to 375 degrees. In a medium bowl, cream sugar and margarine. Add egg and vanilla extract; beat until fluffy. Sift flour, baking powder, and salt together; add to creamed mixture alternately with the milk. Spread batter into a greased and floured 9 inch square pan. In a small bowl, blend all the topping ingredients together and sprinkle on top of batter. Bake for 25 to 35 minutes. Serve warm.

Yield: 9 servings

Note: This is my all-time favorite quick coffee cake. I have prepared it many times. Serve it as a breakfast bread or dessert.

Soups & Salads

 **Soups & Salads**

Soups

Salads

Clam Chowder

2	(6½ ounce) cans clams, reserve juice
2	ounces salt pork, diced
1½	cups diced onions
6	cups diced potatoes
2	small bay leaves, crushed
1	teaspoon salt

¼	teaspoon black pepper
3	cups water
3	tablespoons margarine
2	tablespoons all-purpose flour
4	cups scalded milk
2	cups half-and-half

Strain clams; set clams and juice aside. In a 6 quart stock pot sauté pork until golden browned. Stir in clams; add onions and the next 5 ingredients. Bring to a boil, reduce heat and simmer for approximately 15 minutes. In small saucepan melt margarine; add flour and cook roux about 1 minute; add to stock pot. Measure reserved clam juice and enough water to make 2 cups of liquid. Add clam juice, water, scalded milk, and cream to stock pot. Simmer another 20 minutes.

Yield: 8 to 10 servings

Note: Chowder is a term used for chunky soups or stews that contain seafood, such as clams, with vegetables often added. The term comes from the French word "chaudière," which was long ago Americanized to "chowder."

Seafood Gumbo

1	pound medium shrimp	½	cup scallops, quartered
	Raw celery tops	½	cup sliced okra
2	quarts water		Dash hot pepper sauce
¼	cup diced celery	½	teaspoon Worcestershire sauce
½	cup diced onion	1	small bay leaf
¼	cup diced bell pepper	2	teaspoons salt
1	clove garlic, minced	1½	teaspoons gumbo filé powder
4	tablespoons (½ stick) margarine, divided	½	cup crabmeat
		½	cup whole oysters
1	(14½ ounce) can diced tomatoes	1	cup long-grain rice cooked (optional)
½	cup tomato puree		
3	tablespoons all-purpose flour		

Peel and devein shrimp; wash and save hulls. Place shrimp hulls and a few celery tops into a 4 quart saucepan; add water and boil for about 30 minutes; strain. Sauté celery, onion, bell pepper, and garlic in 2 tablespoons of margarine until tender, but not browned. Add tomatoes, tomato puree, and one quart of the strained stock to the sautéed vegetables. Let simmer for another 30 minutes. Melt the remaining margarine and add flour; cook roux 3 to 4 minutes; do not brown. Stir roux into stock; cook 5 minutes. Add shrimp, scallops, and next 5 ingredients; simmer for 20 minutes. Remove bay leaf. Add the gumbo filé to ½ cup liquid from the pot and blend until smooth. Add mixture to stock and simmer 5 minutes. Remove from heat and stir in crabmeat and oysters. Serve with or without rice.

Yield: 8 servings

Note: Do not let the stock boil after the filé has been added or it will become stringy. Also, blanch the okra in 2 cups of the stock before adding with the seafood and seasonings. If desired, additional crabmeat can be substituted for the oysters.

Corn and Bacon Chowder

6	slices bacon, coarsely diced	1	(10 ounce) package frozen whole kernel corn
1	cup chopped onions		
¾	cup chopped celery	1	(14¾ ounce) can creamed corn
1	large potato, peeled, cut into ½ inch pieces	1	(10½ ounce) can chicken broth
		½	cup chopped celery leaves
2	small bay leaves	¼	teaspoon hot pepper sauce
2	cups milk		Salt and pepper (optional)

Sauté bacon in a 4 quart stock pot over medium heat until crisp and browned. Remove bacon and drain on paper towels. Pour off all but 2 tablespoons drippings from pot. Add onions and celery to pot; sauté about 5 minutes or until tender. Add potato and the next 5 ingredients; bring to boil. Reduce heat to medium-low; cover and simmer chowder until potato is tender, about 15 minutes. Add celery leaves, hot pepper sauce, and bacon. Simmer another 5 minutes. Season with salt and pepper. Remove bay leaves and serve immediately.

Yield: 6 servings

Creamy Squash Soup

4	tablespoons (½ stick) margarine	1	cup milk
1	tablespoon chopped onion	1	bay leaf
2	tablespoons all-purpose flour	2	cups cooked mashed yellow crookneck squash
1	teaspoon salt		
⅛	teaspoon ground nutmeg	1	cup half-and-half
1	(10½ ounce) can chicken broth		

Melt margarine in a 2 quart saucepan over low heat. Add onion and sauté until tender. Blend in flour, salt, and nutmeg; stir until roux bubbles about 2 minutes. Remove from heat, gradually stir in chicken broth and milk. Add bay leaf. Bring to a boil over medium heat; reduce temperature and simmer for 1 minute, stirring constantly. Add squash and half-and-half; heat to serving temperature. Do not boil. Remove bay leaf and serve immediately.

Yield: 4 servings

Creamy Mushroom Soup

1	medium onion, chopped	3	(10¾ ounce) cans beef consommé
2	tablespoons margarine		
¾	pound fresh white mushrooms, sliced	1	cup heavy cream
		⅛	teaspoon ground nutmeg
3	tablespoons all-purpose flour	⅛	teaspoon black pepper

In a 2 quart saucepan, sauté onion in margarine over medium heat until tender. Add mushrooms and cook about 10 minutes. Stir in flour and cook roux about 3 to 4 minutes, stirring constantly. Gradually add consommé and bring to a boil, stirring often. Remove from heat and stir in cream, nutmeg, and pepper. Serve immediately.

Yield: 6 servings

Note: Slice mushrooms lengthwise across the cap and stem. If sliced crosswise they won't hold together when cooked. Store fresh mushrooms in a paper bag or open container in the refrigerator and cover loosely with a slightly damp paper towel.

Pumpkin Soup

1	medium onion, chopped	3	(10½ ounce) cans chicken broth
1	bunch green onions, chopped (white and green parts)	2	cups water
		3	tablespoons all-purpose flour
1	stick plus 3 tablespoons margarine, divided	4	cups half-and-half
			Nutmeg for garnish
1	(15 ounce) can pumpkin		

In a 4 quart saucepan, sauté onions in 1 stick margarine. Do not brown. Stir in pumpkin, chicken broth, and water. Melt the remaining margarine in a small saucepan; add flour and cook roux about 1 minute. Add roux mixture to soup and whisk to blend. Simmer for about 10 minutes. Add the half-and-half just before serving. Garnish with nutmeg.

Yield: 10 to 12 servings

Canadian Cheese Soup

1	carrot	2	ounces Swiss cheese, grated
1	small onion	¼	teaspoon salt
2	ribs celery	¼	teaspoon black pepper
1	stick margarine, divided	½	teaspoon Worcestershire sauce
¼	cup all-purpose flour		Dash of hot pepper sauce
1	quart whole milk	1	(2 ounce) jar chopped
10	ounces processed cheese loaf, sliced		pimientos

Coarsely chop carrot, onion, and celery. Melt 4 tablespoons margarine in a medium saucepan and add the chopped vegetables. Sauté on low heat 10 to 15 minutes or until vegetables are tender. Melt the remaining margarine in a 4 quart saucepan. Add flour and mix well. Cook over low heat 3 to 4 minutes or until the roux is lightly browned, stirring constantly. In another pan scald milk. Add milk to roux mixture and whisk thoroughly. Cook mixture over medium-low heat to thicken. Add cheeses and stir until melted. Add all seasonings, cooked vegetables, and pimientos. Stir to blend the ingredients and serve.

Yield: 6 to 8 servings

Note: Surprise everyone and serve the soup in individual bread bowls. Cut top from round loaves of bread, then hollow them out to make bowls. Brush inside of each with olive oil and toast bowls and lids in a 350 degree oven for 10 minutes or until crusty. Ladle hot soup into the bowls. Place on a plate liner and serve hot.

Chisholm Trail Potato Soup

4	medium potatoes	1	pound processed cheese loaf, sliced
1	stick margarine		Chopped green onions (optional)
6	tablespoons all-purpose flour		
¾	teaspoon black pepper		Crisp bacon, crumbled (optional)
6	cups milk		

Peel and cook potatoes in salted boiling water until tender. Drain and coarsely chop. In a 4 quart saucepan, melt margarine; add flour and pepper; stir until smooth. Cook one minute; stirring constantly. Gradually add milk and whisk to blend; cook over medium heat, stirring constantly until thickened. Add cheese and stir to blend. Add potatoes and heat until mixture reaches serving temperature. Serve soup plain or garnish with chopped green onions and crumbled bacon.

Yield: 8 servings

Southwestern Taco Soup

1½	pounds extra lean ground beef	1	(14 ounce) can pinto beans
1	large onion, chopped	1	(2 ounce) package ranch dressing mix
1	(10 ounce) can diced tomatoes with green chilies	1	(1.25 ounce) package taco seasoning
2	(14½ ounce) cans stewed tomatoes	2	cups water
2	(14¾ ounce) cans whole kernel corn, drained		Cheddar cheese
1	(15 ounce) can kidney beans		Tortilla chips

Brown the ground beef and onions in a 4 quart stock pot. Add all the remaining ingredients and stir to blend. Simmer on low heat for approximately 3 hours. Garnish with grated Cheddar cheese and serve with tortilla chips.

Yield: 8 to 12 servings

Note: This soup has become a favorite in our household. It is easy to prepare and freezes well for serving later.

Italian Vegetable Soup

1	pound lean ground beef	½	teaspoon pepper
1	medium onion, chopped	1	tablespoon chili powder
2	(14½ ounce) cans Italian tomatoes	1	(15 ounce) can kidney beans, drained
1	(10¾ ounce) can tomato soup, undiluted	1	(14½ ounce) can Italian green beans, drained
4	cups water	2	carrots, chopped
2	cloves garlic, minced	1	zucchini, chopped
2	teaspoons dried basil	8	ounces rotini pasta, cooked
2	teaspoons dried oregano		Grated Parmesan cheese
1	teaspoon salt		

Cook beef and onion in a 6 quart stock pot over medium heat, stirring until beef crumbles and is no longer pink; drain. Stir in tomatoes and next 8 ingredients; bring mixture to a boil. Reduce heat and simmer, stirring occasionally, about 30 minutes. Stir in kidney beans and next 3 ingredients; simmer an additional 30 minutes or until vegetables are tender. Stir in pasta. Sprinkle each serving with Parmesan cheese.

Yield: 10 servings

Split Pea Soup with Bacon and Rosemary

4	slices bacon, diced	1¼	cups dried green split peas, rinsed
1	small onion, chopped		
1	rib celery, chopped	2	bay leaves
2	large carrots, chopped	1	teaspoon dried rosemary, crumbled
2	cloves garlic, minced		Salt and pepper
1	(10½ ounce) can chicken broth		
4	cups water		

Sauté bacon in a 3 quart saucepan over medium-high heat until crisp and browned. Add onion, celery, carrots, and garlic; sauté until vegetables begin to soften, about 6 minutes. Add broth and the next 4 ingredients; bring soup to a boil. Reduce heat to medium-low, cover and simmer until peas are tender, about 1 hour; stir occasionally. Remove bay leaves. Season soup with salt and pepper; serve.

Yield: 6 servings

Note: The field pea is a variety of green peas specifically grown for drying. When dried these peas will split along a natural seam which is the origin of their name. Both split peas and lentils are high in fiber.

Lentil and Sausage Soup

6	slices bacon, diced	2	chicken bouillon cubes
1	(16 ounce) package dried lentils, washed	2	bay leaves
1	cup chopped carrots	1	teaspoon salt
1	cup chopped celery	¼	teaspoon pepper
1	medium onion, chopped	7	cups water
2	(14½ ounce) cans diced tomatoes	1	(16 ounce) garlic sausage link

Fry bacon and drain. In a 6 quart stock pot combine the bacon and the next 10 ingredients; stir to mix. Put sausage link on top and simmer for 1 hour or until lentils are tender. Slice sausage and return to soup. Serve hot.

Yield: 8 to 10 servings

Note: Lentils are sometimes used as a meat substitute. They are an excellent source of iron and phosphorus as well as vitamins. This is a hearty soup to serve on a cold winter day. Serve with a good heavy wheat bread for a complete meal. The soup may be frozen and served at a later time without loss of flavor.

Hot Sausage and Bean Stew

1	pound dried pinto beans	1	(14½ ounce) can diced tomatoes
2	teaspoons chili powder	1	fresh jalapeño chili, seeded
1	large onion, chopped		and chopped
1	medium yellow or orange bell pepper, chopped	3	cups hot water
		1	teaspoon salt
2	cloves garlic, minced	1	pound spicy or hot bulk pork
2	tablespoons chopped cilantro		sausage

Check beans, wash, and soak overnight in a large saucepan. Drain beans and place into a large slow cooker. Add all other ingredients except sausage. Lightly brown sausage in a skillet over medium heat; drain off fat. Add browned sausage to bean mixture. Cover and cook on low heat 8 to 9 hours or until beans are tender.

Yield: 8 servings

Note: This recipe may be cooked on top of the stove, using low heat. Increase water to 6 cups. Simmer approximately 3 hours or until beans are tender. If additional water is needed, add hot water. Cold water will cause splitting of beans. If you do not like a lot of pepper, substitute mild sausage for hot sausage.

Jane's Oven Stew

1½	pounds lean stew meat	2	large potatoes, quartered
1	(10¾ ounce) can tomato soup	1	bay leaf
1	(15 ounce) can sweet peas, undrained	1	cup water
		1	teaspoon salt
3	large carrots, sliced	½	teaspoon pepper
1	large onion, chopped		

Place all ingredients into a large covered 4 quart ovenproof casserole. Cook in a 275 degree oven for 6 hours. Remove bay leaf before serving.

Yield: 4 servings

Brown Gravy Stew

1½ pounds lean stew meat
2 tablespoons olive oil
4 cups boiling water
1 tablespoon Worcestershire sauce
1 clove garlic
1 medium onion, chopped
2 bay leaves
1 tablespoon salt

½ teaspoon black pepper
½ teaspoon paprika
⅛ teaspoon ground allspice
6 carrots, cut into chunks
1 large onion, sliced
3 medium potatoes, quartered
2 tablespoons all-purpose flour
¼ cup water

In a 4 quart Dutch oven brown stew meat in olive oil. Add water and next 8 ingredients; simmer for about 2 hours. Remove garlic and bay leaves. Add carrots, onion, and potatoes; cook until vegetables are tender; approximately 30 minutes. Blend flour and water together and add to stew. Simmer about 2 minutes to thicken broth.

Yield: 6 servings

Mixed Greens and Mandarin Orange Salad

Dressing
½ cup olive oil
¼ cup white wine vinegar

2 teaspoons grated orange rind
Salt and pepper

Salad
1 large head of romaine lettuce
1 head red leaf lettuce
1 small red onion, sliced

1 (11 ounce) can mandarin oranges, drained
⅓ cup shelled, roasted, and salted pumpkin seeds

To prepare dressing, whisk oil, vinegar, and orange rind together in a small bowl. Season with salt and pepper; set aside. Tear lettuce into bite-size pieces; add onion and mandarin oranges. Pour dressing over salad and toss to combine ingredients. Sprinkle pumpkin seeds on top of salad just before serving.

Yield: 10 servings

Mixed Greens with Honeyed Almonds

Honeyed Almonds

¼ cup sugar	⅛ teaspoon cayenne
½ teaspoon ground cinnamon	1½ cups whole blanched almonds
¼ teaspoon paprika	1½ tablespoons honey

Vinaigrette Dressing

2½ tablespoons honey	2 tablespoons chopped shallots
⅓ cup red wine vinegar	Salt and pepper
½ cup olive oil	

Salad

1 large head romaine lettuce, torn into bite-size pieces	1 (12 ounce) basket cherry tomatoes, halved
6 cups mixed baby greens	Parmesan cheese

Preheat oven to 350 degrees. Brush rimmed baking sheet with oil. Oil large sheet of foil; set aside. Mix sugar, cinnamon, paprika, and cayenne in medium bowl. Add almonds and honey; toss to coat. Spread out almonds on prepared baking sheet. Bake until almonds are browned and glazed, stirring occasionally, about 15 minutes. Turn almonds out onto oiled foil and cool, separating almonds with fork. For vinaigrette dressing, whisk honey and vinegar in small bowl. Gradually whisk in the oil and mix in shallots. Season with salt and pepper. Set aside. Combine salad greens in a large bowl. Toss with enough vinaigrette to coat. Mound salad on four plates and add tomatoes. Sprinkle with Parmesan cheese and almonds.

Yield: 4 servings

Spinach Salad with Feta Cheese

Dressing

3	tablespoons red wine vinegar
1½	tablespoons olive oil
½	teaspoon salt
¼	teaspoon freshly ground pepper
1	teaspoon sugar

Salad

¾	pound spinach, washed and torn
3	large white mushrooms, thinly sliced
1	small red onion, sliced into rings
¼	pound feta cheese, crumbled

Combine vinegar and all remaining ingredients in a large bowl; whisk to blend. Add spinach, mushrooms, and onions to dressing and toss. Sprinkle with feta cheese.

Yield: 4 servings

Note: Feta cheese was traditionally made from sheep's or goat's milk, however large commercial producers often use cow's milk now to produce this traditional Greek cheese. The rich flavor of the cheese provides a zestful contrast to the spinach in this salad.

Spinach Salad with Raspberry Vinaigrette Dressing

Dressing

¼ cup raspberry vinegar	1½ teaspoons minced onion
½ cup vegetable oil	2 tablespoons sesame seeds
½ cup sugar	2 tablespoons poppy seeds
¼ teaspoon Worcestershire sauce	¼ teaspoon paprika

Salad

2 bags fresh spinach	1 pint fresh strawberries

Combine dressing ingredients in a jar. Shake well to blend flavors. Set aside. Tear spinach into bite-size pieces; wash, hull, and slice strawberries into halves. Toss spinach and strawberries together with dressing.

Yield: 8 servings

Note: This dressing is an excellent choice for use on most fruit salad combinations. It requires only a few minutes to make and will add a fresh made flavor generally not possible with commercial dressings.

Layered Spinach Salad

Salad

2	quarts fresh spinach leaves, washed and torn	1	large yellow or red bell pepper, diced
1	cup broccoli stems, shredded (sold as broccoli coleslaw)	1	(10 ounce) package frozen sweet peas, thawed
2	cups sliced fresh white mushrooms	1	(12 ounce) basket tiny cherry tomatoes, cut in half
1	large red onion, diced		

Topping

3	slices bacon, crumbled	2	teaspoons sugar
¾	cup mayonnaise		Parmesan cheese
¾	cup sour cream		

Layer ½ of the spinach in the bottom of a 2½ quart bowl. Layer the broccoli stems, and the remaining 5 ingredients in the order listed. Add the remaining spinach. Fry bacon until crisp and set aside. Combine mayonnaise, sour cream, and sugar; mix well. Spread evenly over top layer of spinach leaves to seal. Sprinkle crumbled bacon and Parmesan cheese on top of dressing. Cover tightly with plastic wrap and refrigerate until ready to serve.

Yield: 8 to 10 servings

Note: I enjoy serving this salad in a footed glass trifle bowl so the layers of dark green spinach leaves and the other vegetables are visible. It makes an appealing salad when served this way.

Caesar Salad

1	clove garlic, crushed	1	tablespoon Worcestershire sauce
⅔	cup olive oil	1	egg, coddled (1½ minutes)
3	medium heads romaine lettuce, washed	¼	cup fresh lemon juice
1	teaspoon salt	2	tablespoons wine vinegar
	Freshly ground black pepper	½	cup Parmesan cheese
		1	cup croutons

Add garlic to oil and let stand overnight. Tear lettuce into bite-size pieces and place into large salad bowl. Sprinkle with salt, freshly ground pepper, and Worcestershire sauce; toss mixture. Break coddled egg into middle of salad. Pour lemon juice and vinegar over egg; toss lightly to mix well. Remove garlic clove from olive oil and discard. Add olive oil, Parmesan cheese, and croutons to salad; toss and serve.

Yield: 8 servings

Note: Caesar Salad was created at Caesar's Bar and Grill in Tijuana, Mexico. To coddle egg, place enough water into a small saucepan to cover the egg. Bring water to boil and remove from heat. Gently place egg into covered pan and cook 1½ minutes.

Layered Chicken-Avocado-Cheese Salad

Dressing

3	tablespoons red wine vinegar	½	teaspoon salt
1	tablespoon fresh lemon juice	½	teaspoon sugar
2	teaspoons creamy mustard blend	¼	teaspoon black pepper
1	small clove garlic, minced	½	cup olive oil

Salad

1-1¼	pounds skinless boneless chicken breast, cooked	3	tomatoes, cut into ½ inch pieces
2	avocados	4	ounces Roquefort cheese, crumbled
1	head romaine lettuce, washed	2	hard boiled eggs, forced through a coarse sieve
6	slices bacon, cooked, drained, crumbled	¼	cup finely chopped fresh chives

In a small bowl, whisk together all dressing ingredients except oil. Add oil in a slow stream, whisking until emulsified. Set aside. Cut chicken into ½-inch cubes; set aside. Peel, pit, and cut avocados into ½-inch cubes. Tear lettuce into bite-size pieces and spread over bottom of a 6 quart or larger glass bowl; top with a layer of chicken; sprinkle with bacon. Continue layering with tomatoes, cheese, avocados, eggs, and chives. Cover and chill until ready to serve. To serve, pour dressing over salad and toss.

Yield: 6 to 8 servings

Mexican Salad

1	pound lean ground beef	1	bunch green onion, chopped (white and green parts)
1	(1.25 ounce) package taco seasoning mix	2	cups (8 ounces) grated Cheddar cheese
1	(10 ounce) can tomatoes and green chilies		Tortilla chips (optional)
1	head iceberg lettuce, chopped		Guacamole (optional)
2	medium tomatoes, chopped		Sour cream (optional)

In a large skillet, brown ground beef on medium-high heat until no longer pink; drain well. Stir in taco seasoning mix and tomatoes and green chilies. Simmer mixture until liquid has evaporated; set aside to cool. In a large bowl, combine lettuce, tomatoes, onions and cheese. Add meat mixture and gently toss salad. Serve with tortilla chips, guacamole, and sour cream, if desired.

Yield: 6 to 8 servings

Note: Recipe for Chunky Guacamole Dip is located on page 9. Omit chopped tomatoes if preparing recipe to use with Mexican Salad.

Cucumber Cooler

4	cucumbers, peeled and sliced	2	tablespoons cider vinegar
1	red onion, thinly sliced and separated	½	teaspoon salt
½	cup sour cream	½	teaspoon pepper

Combine cucumbers and onion in a large bowl. In a small bowl, mix remaining ingredients and pour over cucumber mixture; stir mixture to evenly coat cucumbers and onions. Refrigerate for several hours before serving.

Yield: 6 to 8 servings

Country-Style Coleslaw

½	cup mayonnaise	4	cups shredded cabbage
2	tablespoons sugar	¾	cup grated carrots
2	tablespoons cider vinegar	¼	cup diced bell pepper
¾	teaspoon salt	¼	cup sliced green onions (white and green parts)
¼	teaspoon dry mustard		
⅛	teaspoon celery seeds		

In a large bowl, combine the mayonnaise, and the next five ingredients; whisk ingredients together to blend. Add the cabbage, carrots, pepper, and onions; toss ingredients to coat well. Cover; chill at least 2 hours before serving.

Yield: 8 servings

German Coleslaw

Slaw

1	head cabbage	1	(4 ounce) jar diced pimientos, drained
¼	cup chopped bell pepper		

Dressing

¾	cup vinegar	½	teaspoon coarsely ground black pepper
¾	cup salad oil		
1½	teaspoons salt		

Shred cabbage and mix with bell pepper and pimientos; set aside. Place dressing ingredients into a small bowl and whisk to blend. Pour dressing over cabbage and mix well. Cover and place in refrigerator to allow flavors to blend before serving.

Yield: 8 to 10 servings

Note: This coleslaw is best made with a vinegar that has a high acidity content. It complements most meats and will keep several days. It is especially good served with grilled hamburgers.

Green Pea Salad

2   (15 ounce) cans sweet peas,
     drained
1   cup diced celery
4   ounces American cheese, diced
½   cup diced sweet pickles

1   (2 ounce) jar, diced pimientos,
     drained
½   cup mayonnaise
     Salt and pepper (optional)

In a medium bowl combine the peas and the next 4 ingredients. Add mayonnaise and toss lightly to coat ingredients. Season with salt and pepper. Cover and refrigerate for 2 hours or more before serving.

Yield: 8 servings

Broccoli Salad

Salad

12 slices thin bacon
1   large bunch broccoli florets
1   cup green grapes, sliced in half

½   cup diced red onion
⅓   cup roasted sunflower seeds

Dressing

1   cup mayonnaise
¼   cup sugar

2   tablespoons red wine vinegar

Cook bacon until crisp; drain; crumble and set aside. Wash broccoli and separate into small florets. Toss broccoli, grapes, onion, sunflower seeds, and bacon together. Blend dressing ingredients together and add to salad. Refrigerate overnight or serve immediately.

Yield: 6 to 8 servings

Note: For a larger salad double the recipe. If you prefer, you can substitute white or dark raisins for the grapes. If you are calorie conscience, reduce the amount of bacon in the recipe.

Harvest Salad

Salad

2	broccoli bunches	4	large carrots, grated
1	cauliflower	1	medium red onion, chopped

Dressing

1½	cups mayonnaise	1	pound thick sliced bacon
¾	cup sugar	¾	cup Parmesan cheese
3	tablespoons tarragon vinegar		

Cut the broccoli and cauliflower into bite-size florets; place into large mixing bowl. Add the carrots and onion. In a small bowl combine mayonnaise, sugar, and vinegar. Toss salad with dressing and place into a 2 quart serving bowl. Cook bacon until crisp; crumble and sprinkle on salad with Parmesan cheese. Refrigerate 2 hours or more before serving. Toss salad well before serving.

Yield: 12 or more servings

Confetti Corn Salad

Salad

1 (15 ounce) can whole kernel corn	¼ cup chopped bell pepper
¼ cup chopped red onion	¼ cup chopped red bell pepper

Dressing

¼ cup vegetable oil	1 teaspoon sugar
¼ cup apple cider vinegar	½ teaspoon salt
1½ teaspoons lemon juice	⅛ teaspoon cayenne
¼ cup chopped fresh cilantro	½ teaspoon garlic salt

Drain the whole kernel corn; mix with the onion and peppers. Combining all dressing ingredients in a jar and shake to blend. Add dressing to salad and stir to combine all ingredients. Cover and chill for several hours or overnight before serving.

Yield: 6 servings

Note: For a festive look, serve this salad in tomato shells. Cut ½ inch from the top of 6 large tomatoes and scoop out the seeds and pulp with a teaspoon. Sprinkle the shells with salt and pepper and drain inverted on paper towels for a few minutes. Fill each tomato shell with ½ cup of the chilled corn mixture.

Shoepeg Corn Salad

Salad

1 (14½ ounce) can French-style beans, drained	1 cup chopped celery
1 (11 ounce) can shoepeg corn, drained	1 bunch green onions, chopped (white and green parts)
1 (15 ounce) can sweet peas, drained	1 (2 ounce) jar diced pimientos
	1 bell pepper, chopped

Dressing

1 cup sugar	¾ cup vinegar
½ cup vegetable oil	Salt and pepper

Combine vegetables in a large bowl and set aside. Mix dressing ingredients together in a small saucepan and heat to boiling. Pour dressing over vegetables and stir to mix. Spoon salad into a 2 quart serving dish and refrigerate for 24 hours before serving.

Yield: 10 to 12 servings

Note: Shoepeg is a small, cream colored corn with slender kernels. If you are unable to locate shoepeg corn, use white corn for this recipe.

Apricot Mousse

1 (6 ounce) package apricot flavored gelatin	2 (4 ounce) jars apricot baby food
¾ cup sugar	1 (8 ounce) package cream cheese, softened
1 (20 ounce) can crushed pineapple, undrained	1 (12 ounce) can evaporated milk, chilled

Combine gelatin, sugar, and pineapple, in a 2 quart saucepan; heat until gelatin has dissolved. Set aside to cool. Blend apricot baby food and cream cheese together; fold into the cooled gelatin mixture. Refrigerate until slightly thickened. Whip the evaporated milk and fold into gelatin mixture. Pour into 13 x 9 inch baking dish and chill until firm. Cut into squares to serve.

Yield: 12 servings

Congealed Ambrosia Salad

Salad

1 (15¼ ounce) can pineapple
   tidbits, drained, reserve juice
1 (11 ounce) cans Mandarin
   oranges, drained, reserve juice

1 (6 ounce) package orange
   flavored gelatin
2 cups orange sherbet

Fruit Mixture

1 (11 ounce) can Mandarin
   oranges, drained
1 cup flaked coconut

1 cup miniature marshmallows
1 cup sour cream

Drain pineapple and Mandarin oranges; reserve juice. Add enough water to juice to measure 2 cups. Heat juice and water to boiling; add gelatin and stir until dissolved. Remove from heat and add sherbet; stir until sherbet melts. Chill until partially set; add pineapple and oranges. Spoon mixture into lightly oiled 6 cup ring mold. Cover and chill until firm. Combine oranges, coconut, marshmallows, and sour cream; stir to mix. Chill mixture until ready to serve. Unmold salad onto lettuce-lined plate; spoon fruit mixture into center and serve.

Yield: 10 to 12 servings

Note: To unmold a congealed salad, loosen edge with a knife to release the vacuum. Dip in warm water for a few seconds and invert onto a chilled plate.

Congealed Blackberry Salad

1 (8¼ ounce) can crushed
   pineapple, undrained
1 (6 ounce) package blackberry
   flavored gelatin

2 cups buttermilk
1 (10 ounce) carton frozen
   nondairy whipped topping

Heat pineapple in a 2 quart saucepan over medium-high heat until boiling; add gelatin; continue heating until gelatin dissolves, about 1 minute. Set aside until mixture is completely cooled. Add buttermilk and whipped topping. Spoon mixture into a 6 cup mold. Chill until firm. Unmold and serve.

Yield: 6 to 8 servings

Maggie's Cranberry Salad

1	pound cranberries	3	cups boiling water
½	cup sugar	1	cup chopped celery
1	orange (grated rind only)	1	(8¼ ounce) can crushed pineapple, undrained
1	(6 ounce) package cherry flavored gelatin	1	cup chopped pecans

Finely chop cranberries in food processor; add sugar. Grate rind of orange; add to cranberries and sugar. Refrigerate for several hours or overnight. Dissolve gelatin in water. Combine gelatin and remaining ingredients with cranberry mixture. Spoon into 13 x 9 inch dish. Chill until firm. Cut into squares to serve.

Yield: 10 to 12 servings

Note: Cranberry dishes are traditionally served during the Christmas or Thanksgiving holidays, however you may want to serve this salad at other times. The flavor of the tart berries and orange is especially good with chicken dishes.

Cranberry Sour Cream Swirl Salad

1	(6 ounce) package red raspberry gelatin	1	(20 ounce) can crushed pineapple, undrained
1½	cups boiling water	1	cup sour cream
1	(16 ounce) can whole cranberry sauce		

Dissolve gelatin in water. Whisk cranberry sauce to break apart. Add cranberry sauce and undrained pineapple to gelatin. Chill until partially set. Spoon into 11 x 7 inch dish. Spoon sour cream on top and stir to swirl. Chill until firm. Cut into squares to serve.

Yield: 8 servings

Note: Cranberries are one of only three major fruits native to North America. The other two are blueberries and Concord grapes. In addition to cranberry sauce, this fruit makes delicious chutney, pies, and cobblers. Since cranberries are so very tart they are best combined with sweeter fruits.

Double Lemon Salad

1 (6 ounce) package lemon flavored gelatin	1 (20 ounce) can crushed pineapple, undrained
2 cups boiling water	1 cup sour cream
½ cup cold water	3 tablespoons powdered sugar
1 (21 ounce) can lemon pie filling	

Add gelatin to boiling water and stir until dissolved; add cold water. Add pie filling and whisk until well blended. Stir in pineapple and blend. Pour mixture into a 13 x 9 inch baking dish and chill until firm. Blend sour cream and powdered sugar together; spread on top of congealed gelatin. Chill. Cut into squares to serve.

Yield: 10 to 12 servings

Note: This refreshing salad can also be served as a dessert. Bake up a batch of sugar cookies using the recipe found on page 222 to serve with this salad for an extra treat.

Divinity Salad

1 (6 ounce) package lemon flavored gelatin	¾ cup chopped pecans
¾ cup boiling water	1 (20 ounce) can crushed pineapple, undrained
1 (8 ounce) package cream cheese, softened	1 (10 ounce) carton frozen nondairy whipped topping
2 tablespoons sugar	

Dissolve gelatin in water. Set aside to cool. Add cream cheese to cooled gelatin and whisk until well blended. Add sugar, pecans, and pineapple. Refrigerate until mixture is slightly thickened; fold in whipped topping. Pour mixture into a 13 x 9 inch dish. Chill until firm. Cut into squares to serve.

Yield: 12 servings

Carolyn's Lime Gelatin Salad

1   (8¼ ounce) can crushed
    pineapple
1   (3 ounce) package lime
    flavored gelatin
1   avocado

1   (3 ounce) package cream
    cheese, softened
½   cup chopped pecans
1   package whipped topping mix

Drain pineapple and reserve juice. Add enough water with pineapple juice to measure 1½ cups. Heat liquid to boiling; add gelatin and stir until dissolved. Set aside to cool. Fold in crushed pineapple. Peel and mash avocado; blend with cream cheese and add to gelatin mixture. Stir in pecans. Gently fold in whipped topping mix, prepared according to directions on package. Spoon mixture into a 11 x 7 inch dish and chill until firm. Cut into squares to serve.

Yield: 8 servings

Red Raspberry Mold

1   (6 ounce) package raspberry
    flavored gelatin
2   cups boiling water
2   cups vanilla ice cream

1   (10 ounce) package frozen red
    raspberries, thawed, reserve
    syrup
1   (6 ounce) can frozen pink
    lemonade concentrate, thawed

Dissolve gelatin in water; add ice cream and stir to blend. Combine raspberry syrup and lemonade with gelatin mixture. Chill until slightly thickened; add raspberries. Spoon mixture into a 2 quart mold or an 8 inch square baking dish. Chill until firm. Cut into squares to serve.

Yield: 8 servings

Congealed Strawberry Salad

1 (6 ounce) package strawberry flavored gelatin
2 cups boiling water
1 (10 ounce) package frozen strawberries, thawed

1 (8¼ ounce) can crushed pineapple, undrained
3 large bananas, chopped fine
1 cup sour cream

Dissolve gelatin in water; cool mixture. Add strawberries, pineapple, and bananas. Pour into a 13 x 9 baking dish and chill until firm. Spread sour cream over top. Cut into squares for serving.

Yield: 8 to 10 servings

Festive Molded Fruit

1 (20 ounce) can pineapple chunks, reserve juice
1 (15 ounce) can pitted Bing cherries, reserve juice
2 (6 ounce) packages strawberry flavored gelatin

2 (16 ounce) cans whole cranberry sauce
1 (16 ounce) bag whole strawberries, partially defrosted

Drain pineapple chunks and cherries; reserve juice and add enough water to make 2 cups. Heat juice and water to boiling; add gelatin and stir to dissolve. Add cranberry sauce to gelatin mixture and whisk to blend; fold in pineapple chunks and cherries. Chill until partially set and add strawberries. Spoon mixture into a 13 x 9 inch dish and refrigerate until congealed. Cut into squares for serving.

Yield: 15 or more servings

Pistachio Cloud Salad

1	(3 ounce) package pistachio instant pudding	1	(10 ounce) carton frozen nondairy whipped topping
1	(20 ounce) can crushed pineapple, undrained	2	cups miniature marshmallows
		½	cup chopped pecans

Combine pudding mix and pineapple in a large bowl; stir until thick. Add whipped topping and stir to blend. Fold in marshmallows and pecans. Refrigerate until serving time.

Yield: 8 to 10 servings

Note: This recipe has been around a long time and goes by many names. I usually serve it as a dessert. It makes a great buffet dish for special occasions.

Frozen Fruit Salad

1	(15¼ ounce) can fruit cocktail	2	tablespoons lemon juice
1	(11 ounce) can Mandarin oranges	½	cup mayonnaise
1	(3 ounce) package lemon flavored gelatin	1	cup miniature marshmallows
		½	cup heavy cream

Drain fruit cocktail and Mandarin oranges, reserve juice; add enough water to juice to make 1 cup. Heat juice and water to boiling and stir in gelatin; stir until dissolved. Add lemon juice and chill until partially set. Fold in fruit cocktail, orange sections, mayonnaise, and marshmallows. Whip cream and fold into mixture. Spoon into 8 individual molds or an 8 inch square dish. Freeze until firm. Cut into squares to serve.

Yield: 8 servings

Note: You may want to serve this fruit salad as a dessert. Substitute ½ cup sour cream for the mayonnaise and refrigerate until firm enough to cut into squares.

Tropical Fruit Salad

Salad

1	(20 ounce) can pineapple chunks
1	(11 ounce) can Mandarin oranges

2	kiwi fruits
1	cup strawberries
2	bananas, sliced
½	cup shredded coconut

Fruit Dressing

½	cup sugar
1½	tablespoons cornstarch
½	cup juice from drained fruit
1	small lemon, grated rind

1	small orange, grated rind
2	tablespoons lemon juice
2	tablespoons orange juice

Drain canned fruit; set aside fruit and juice. Wash, peel, and slice kiwi fruits: wash and slice strawberries; slice bananas. In a large bowl, combine all fruits and coconut, toss together and set aside. In a small saucepan mix sugar and cornstarch; add fruit juice and stir to blend. Cook, stirring constantly, until mixture thickens and boils, about 1 minute. Remove from heat and stir in remaining ingredients. Chill dressing and toss with fruit just before serving.

Yield: 8 servings

Note: Kiwi fruits are generally available year around since they are cultivated both in California and New Zealand. The sweet-tart flavor is unlike any other fruit and blends well with most fruits. Store ripe kiwis in the refrigerator.

Creamy Fruit Salad

1	(20 ounce) can sliced peaches	⅓	cup maraschino cherries, cut in half
1	(20 ounce) can pineapple chunks	1	(3 ounce) package instant vanilla or lemon pudding mix
1	(11 ounce) can Mandarin oranges	⅓	cup grated coconut
		3	bananas, sliced

Drain fruit well, reserving 1½ cups juice. In a large bowl mix juice and pudding mix together; whisk until mixture thickens. Fold peaches, pineapple, oranges, cherries, and coconut into pudding mixture. Refrigerate fruit mixture until well chilled. Add bananas and spoon salad into a 1½ quart serving dish just before serving.

Yield: 8 to 10 servings

Overnight Fruit Salad

1	(8¼ ounce) can pineapple chunks, drained	1	cup miniature marshmallows
1	(11 ounce) can Mandarin oranges, drained	1	cup coconut
		1	cup sour cream

Drain pineapple and Mandarin oranges. Combine all ingredients and stir to mix. Spoon mixture into a 1½ quart dish and refrigerate overnight.

Yield: 6 servings

Fruit Cup

1 (16 ounce) package whole
   frozen strawberries
1 (16 ounce) package sliced
   frozen peaches

1 cup fresh blueberries
1 (20 ounce) can pineapple
   chunks, drained
2 bananas sliced

Partially thaw the strawberries and peaches; combine with the remaining ingredients and allow fruits to thaw before serving.

Yield: 10 to 12 servings

Festive Holiday Fruit Salad

Sauce

2 eggs, beaten
¼ cup vinegar

¼ cup sugar
2 tablespoons margarine

Fruit Mixture

1 (16½ ounce) can Royal Ann
   cherries, drained
2 (11 ounce) cans Mandarin
   oranges, drained
1 (20 ounce) can pineapple
   chunks, drained

1 (15¼ ounce) can peaches, cut
   into ½ inch pieces
2 cups miniature marshmallows
1 cup heavy cream, whipped

In a double boiler mix eggs, vinegar, and sugar together. Cook over low heat until mixture is thick and smooth. Remove from heat; add margarine and allow to cool. In a large bowl, combine the fruit and sauce; fold in marshmallows and cream. Spoon salad into a 2½ quart serving bowl. Refrigerate salad overnight before serving.

Yield: 12 or more servings

Waldorf Salad

2	medium apples	1	(8¼ ounce) can pineapple
2	ribs celery, chopped		chunks, drained
⅓	cup raisins	½	cup miniature marshmallows
½	cup walnuts, chopped	½	cup mayonnaise
			Lettuce cups (optional)

Core the apples and cut them into ½ inch pieces. In a large bowl, combine the apples and next 5 ingredients. Add mayonnaise and toss to blend. Spoon mixture into a 1½ quart serving dish or serve in lettuce cups.

Yield: 6 to 8 servings

Note: The original version of this popular fruit salad was created at New York's famed Waldorf-Astoria Hotel in 1896. At first, the salad contained only apples, celery, and mayonnaise. Walnuts were added later.

Pasta Salad with Corn and Cheese

1	(15¼ ounce) can whole kernel corn, drained, reserve liquid	1	cup Parmesan cheese
4	quarts water	2	cups mayonnaise
1	tablespoon salt	1	bunch green onions, chopped (white and green parts)
1	(16 ounce) package fettuccine pasta	1	red bell pepper, diced
2	chicken bouillon cubes, crushed	1	tablespoon black pepper
		1	teaspoon garlic powder

Drain corn and add liquid to water in a large stock pot. Add salt to liquid and bring to a boil before adding fettuccine. Reduce heat and simmer about 5 to 7 minutes. Drain and rinse with cold water; set aside. Combine all remaining ingredients in a microwave-safe dish and cook on full power about 1 minute until warm. Stir to blend. Pour sauce over fettuccine and toss to combine ingredients. Spoon mixture into a 2½ quart serving dish and serve immediately or chill before serving.

Yield: 10 to 12 servings

Beverely's Italian Pasta Salad

Salad

8	ounces rotini pasta	4	ounces salami or pepperoni, chopped
1	(4 ounce) can black olives, drained, sliced	4	ounces Monterey Jack cheese
4	ounces mushrooms, sliced	2	medium zucchini
1	red bell pepper, chopped	1	(12 ounce) basket cherry tomatoes, halved
1	bunch green onions, chopped (white and green parts)	¼	cup Parmesan cheese
½	cup chopped fresh parsley		

Dressing

2	cloves garlic, minced	1	teaspoon sugar
¾	teaspoon dried oregano	1	teaspoon salt
¼	teaspoon dried rosemary	½	teaspoon black pepper
2	tablespoons dried basil	⅓	cup red wine vinegar
¼	teaspoon dried tarragon	½	cup olive oil

Cook pasta according to package directions; rinse in cold water and drain. Place pasta into a large bowl and combine with olives and next 5 ingredients. Grate cheese and zucchini; add to pasta. Add tomatoes and Parmesan cheese; toss to mix thoroughly; set aside. To prepare dressing, mix garlic and dry ingredients together in a small bowl. Add vinegar and olive oil and whisk to blend. Pour dressing over salad and toss to mix. Spoon mixture into a 3 quart serving dish and refrigerate until ready to serve.

Yield: 10 to 12 servings

Note: To prevent over cooking pasta, test for doneness at the shortest cooking time. It should be cooked until just tender. If desired, substitute ¾ cup of commercial Italian dressing for this dressing recipe.

Italian Pasta Salad

Dressing

½ cup olive oil	1 teaspoon salt
¼ cup white wine vinegar	½ teaspoon sugar
1 teaspoon freshly ground pepper	1 clove garlic

Salad

1 (16 ounce) package penne pasta	1 (4 ounce) can black olives, drained, sliced
4 ounces pepperoni, cubed	
4 ounces feta cheese, crumbled	¼ cup chopped fresh parsley
1 bunch green onions, chopped (white and green parts)	Parmesan cheese.

Prepare dressing by combining all ingredients in a jar. Shake jar well and set aside while preparing salad. Cook pasta according to package directions; rinse in cold water and drain. Toss drained pasta with all the remaining salad ingredients, except the Parmesan cheese. Remove garlic clove from dressing; pour dressing over salad and toss well. Spoon salad into a 2½ quart serving dish and sprinkle with Parmesan cheese.

Yield: 8 servings

Red Potatoes and Onion Salad

4 pounds red potatoes	2 cups ranch dressing with bacon
½ pound bacon	
1 bunch green onions, chopped (white and green parts)	Paprika

Scrub potatoes and cook in salted boiling water until tender; cool and slice into chunks. Cook bacon until crisp; drain and crumble. Combine all ingredients and toss to coat potatoes; spoon mixture into a 3 quart serving bowl. Sprinkle with paprika.

Yield: 8 to 10 servings

Note: This is a little different kind of potato salad than the usual, but it is delicious. Any time I serve this salad, I have requests for the recipe.

Country Potato Salad

5	medium potatoes	½	cup mayonnaise
2	teaspoons salt	2	teaspoons prepared yellow mustard
4	hard-boiled eggs	½	teaspoon salt
½	cup sweet pickle relish	½	teaspoon pepper
1	small onion, chopped	¼	cup sweet pickle juice
1	(2 ounce) jar chopped pimientos, drained	½	teaspoon garlic powder
1	tablespoon dried parsley		Paprika
2	ribs celery, chopped		

Place potatoes in a large stock pot; cover with water and add salt. Bring water to boiling; reduce temperature and simmer potatoes until done. Cool and cut potatoes into ½ inch cubes. Cut boiled eggs into cubes and add to potatoes; set aside. In a small bowl, combine the pickle relish and the next 10 ingredients; add mixture to potatoes and toss. Spoon salad into a 2 quart serving dish and sprinkle with paprika. Refrigerate until ready to serve.

Yield: 8 servings

Note: Potato salad is almost as American as apple pie. It is a standard side dish served with barbecue in Texas. Although recipes for this popular side dish vary, I believe you will enjoy serving this one to your family and guests often.

Tuna Salad

1	(12 ounce) can albacore tuna, drained, flaked	½	cup pickle relish
¾	cup chopped celery	½	cup mayonnaise
1	Red Delicious apple, chopped		Salt and pepper
			Lettuce cups

In a medium bowl, combine the tuna and the next 4 ingredients. Season with salt and pepper. Spoon salad into lettuce cups and serve.

Yield: 4 servings

Note: If preparing this salad to use as a sandwich spread, chop celery and apple extra fine. Any variety of tuna may be used in this recipe, however I prefer the albacore packed in water. It has the lightest flesh of all tuna and is mild flavored.

Vegetables & Side Dishes

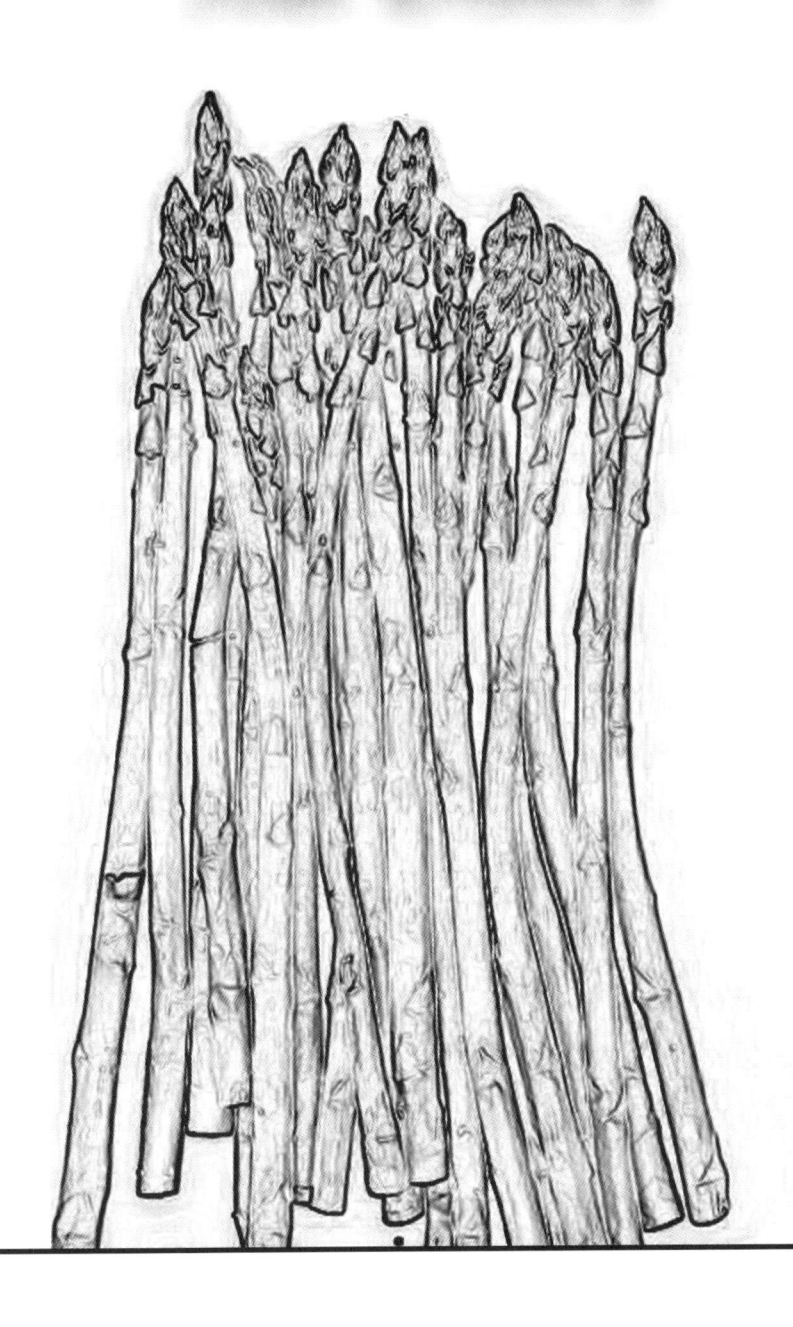

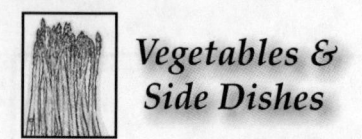
Vegetables &
Side Dishes

Vegetables

Side Dishes

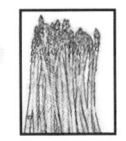

Corn Casserole

1	bunch green onions, chopped (white and green parts)	1	egg, beaten
1	bell pepper, chopped	1	(6 ounce) package corn bread mix
1	stick margarine	1	cup grated Cheddar cheese
1	(14 ounce) can cream-style corn	1	(2 ounce) jar diced pimientos, drained
1	(11 ounce) can whole kernel corn, drained		

Preheat oven to 350 degrees. In a small dish, cover and cook onions, pepper, and margarine in a microwave oven on high power for 3 minutes or until tender. In a large bowl, combine corn and the next 4 ingredients; stir in onions and pepper. Spoon mixture into a greased 2 quart casserole dish; bake for 45 minutes or until lightly browned.

Yield: 6 to 8 servings

Note: This is an excellent casserole that is easy to prepare. I frequently include this dish as part of our Thanksgiving dinner and the guys love it.

Broccoli Corn Casserole

1	(10 ounce) package frozen chopped broccoli	1	(10¾ ounce) can cream of mushroom soup, undiluted
1	(10 ounce) package cream-style corn	1	egg, beaten
1¼	cups herb-seasoned stuffing mix, divided	3	tablespoons margarine, melted
		1	small onion, finely chopped
		½	cup (2 ounces) grated sharp Cheddar cheese

Preheat oven to 350 degrees. Cook broccoli according to package directions, omitting salt; drain. Cook corn according to package directions. In a large bowl, combine the broccoli and corn; add 1 cup stuffing mix and the next 4 ingredients; mix well. Spoon mixture into a greased 1½ quart baking dish. Sprinkle with cheese and remaining stuffing mix. Bake for 30 minutes or until thoroughly heated.

Yield: 6 servings

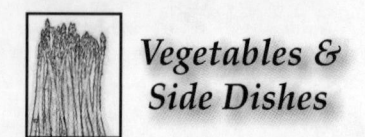

Squash Soufflé

4	pounds yellow squash, sliced	1½	cups bread crumbs
½	cup chopped onion	1	teaspoon salt
4	tablespoons (½ stick) margarine	¼	teaspoon black pepper
1	(2 ounce) jar diced pimientos, drained	2	eggs, beaten

Preheat oven to 350 degrees. In a large saucepan, cook squash in salted boiling water until tender. Drain squash and mash or chop fine. In a small saucepan sauté onion in margarine until tender, but not browned. Add onion, pimientos, bread crumbs, salt, and pepper to squash. Add eggs and blend thoroughly; spoon into a greased 8 inch square baking dish. Bake for 30 minutes or until browned.

Yield: 8 servings

Note: There are many varieties of squash, but none are as popular as yellow squash. Archeological evidence suggests squash was eaten in Mexico as early as 5500 B.C. which, I suppose, proves this native of the Americas has real staying power!

Sweet-Sour Cabbage

5	cups shredded cabbage	3	tablespoons light brown sugar
6	slices bacon, diced	¼	cup vinegar
1	small onion, chopped	½	cup water
3	tablespoons all-purpose flour		Salt and pepper

Cook cabbage in salted boiling water 5 minutes or until tender; drain and set aside. Cook bacon until crisp; add to cabbage. Sauté onion in bacon fat until tender; add flour and brown sugar and stir to blend. Add vinegar and water; cook until sauce thickens. Pour sauce over cabbage and stir to blend. Season with salt and pepper. Heat thoroughly and serve.

Yield: 4 servings

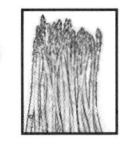

Mushroom Casserole

1   egg yolk
1   cup half-and-half, divided
1   stick margarine, divided
1½ pounds white mushrooms, sliced
3   tablespoons all-purpose flour

1   tablespoon chopped fresh parsley
½   lemon (juice only)
¼   teaspoon paprika
1   cup crushed buttery round crackers

Preheat oven to 350 degrees. Beat together egg yolk and 2 tablespoons half-and-half; set aside. Melt 4 tablespoons margarine in a large pan and sauté mushrooms until golden. Stir in flour and parsley. Reduce heat to low and add remaining half-and-half, lemon juice, and paprika; stir to blend. Add egg yolk and cream mixture; blend thoroughly. Spoon mixture into a greased 1 quart casserole. Melt remaining margarine and mix with cracker crumbs; sprinkle crumbs on casserole. Bake for 30 minutes or until top is lightly browned.

Yield: 6 servings

Note: The most common mushroom found in supermarkets is the cultivated white mushroom. The cap of this one ranges in size from ½ to 3 inches across, and the color will vary from white to pale tan. With age, these mushrooms often darken and loose firmness. If you enjoy the flavor of mushrooms as I do, try this casserole.

Carrots and Pineapple

1 (16 ounce) package baby carrots	1 tablespoon light brown sugar
1¼ cups water, divided	1 tablespoon margarine
½ teaspoon salt	⅛ teaspoon ground nutmeg
1 (8¼ ounce) can crushed pineapple, undrained	1½ teaspoons cornstarch

In a medium saucepan, combine carrots with 1 cup water and salt; bring to boil. Reduce heat; cover and simmer until carrots are tender, about 10 minutes. Drain carrots; return to pan. Add the pineapple, sugar, margarine, and nutmeg. Mix cornstarch into the remaining water; add to carrot mixture. Cook, stirring constantly until sauce thickens. Serve immediately.

Yield: 4 to 6 servings

Note: Choose carrots with care. The fresher the better! Carrots should be firm and smooth when purchased. Avoid carrots with cracks or any that are soft. Carrots that are limp can be restored to crispness by soaking them a few minutes in ice water.

Holiday Peas

1 (10 ounce) package frozen sweet peas	1½ tablespoons margarine
1 small onion, chopped	1 (2 ounce) jar diced pimientos, drained
½ cup chopped celery	½ teaspoon salt
1 cup sliced white mushrooms	⅛ teaspoon black pepper

Cook the peas in the microwave oven, according to the package directions. Drain off any liquid. In a medium-size skillet, sauté the onion, celery, and mushrooms in margarine. Add the cooked peas, pimientos, salt, and pepper; stir to combine and heat thoroughly. Serve immediately.

Yield: 6 servings

Carrot Pudding

3	eggs, separated	3	tablespoons margarine
¼	cup sugar	1	teaspoon salt
1	cup milk, divided	1	cup fine bread crumbs
1½	tablespoons cornstarch	1	cup half-and-half
3	cups (2 pounds) carrots, cooked, drained, and mashed	½	teaspoon ground nutmeg

Preheat oven to 300 degrees. In a small bowl, beat the egg yolks and sugar until light; set aside. In a large saucepan blend 1/4 cup of milk and cornstarch to make a paste; add remaining milk and stir to blend. Cook over medium heat until the sauce is smooth and slightly thickened. Stir small amount of the hot cornstarch sauce into egg yolk mixture and blend; add egg mixture to cornstarch sauce and cook over medium heat until smooth and thick. Add carrots, margarine, salt, and bread crumbs; stir to combine. Stir in half-and-half and nutmeg. Beat egg whites until they hold firm peaks; fold into carrot mixture. Spoon mixture into a greased 2 quart casserole dish. Place casserole dish into a pan filled with 1 inch of hot water and bake for 30 minutes. Increase heat to 350 degrees and bake an additional 45 minutes, or until knife inserted into center comes out clean.

Yield: 10 to 12 servings

Wilted Greens

1 large bunch Swiss chard	1 (10 ounce) bag spinach leaves
1 large bunch mustard greens	⅓ cup canned chicken broth
3 tablespoons margarine	Salt and pepper

Wash the Swiss chard and mustard greens; remove tough stems and discard; tear leaves into pieces. In a 3 quart saucepan, melt margarine over medium-high heat. Add all greens and chicken broth. Cover and cook until greens wilt, stirring occasionally, about 3 minutes. Uncover and cook until juices thicken slightly, about 4 minutes. Season with salt and pepper.

Yield: 4 servings

Note: The flavor of this dish comes from the balance of three popular greens. Spinach and mustard greens are the best known, but Swiss chard should not be overlooked. Swiss chard is a member of the beet family and is a good source of vitamins A and C, and iron.

Corn and Rice Casserole

1 large onion, chopped	1 (2 ounce) jar chopped pimientos, drained
1 small bell pepper, chopped	
1 stick margarine	2 teaspoons sugar
2 (14¾ ounce) cans cream-style corn	1 egg, beaten
	Salt and pepper
2 cups instant rice, uncooked	1 cup grated Cheddar cheese
	Paprika

Preheat oven to 350 degrees. In a small skillet over medium-high heat, sauté onion and pepper in margarine until tender, but not browned. In a large mixing bowl, blend corn, rice, pimientos, and sugar. Stir in egg, onion, and bell pepper. Season with salt and pepper. Spoon mixture into a greased 2 quart casserole and sprinkle with cheese and paprika. Bake uncovered for 30 minutes or until browned.

Yield: 6 to 8 servings

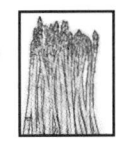

Scalloped Corn and Tomatoes

2	(14½ ounce) cans diced tomatoes	2	teaspoons sugar
1	(15¼ ounce) can whole kernel corn, drained	½	teaspoon black pepper
		1	medium onion, finely chopped
1	(14¾ ounce) can cream-style corn	4	tablespoons (½ stick) margarine
		½	teaspoon garlic powder
2	slightly beaten eggs	4	cups soft bread crumbs
¼	cup all-purpose flour	½	cup Parmesan cheese

Preheat oven to 350 degrees. In a large bowl, combine tomatoes and the next 6 ingredients. Spoon mixture into a greased 2 quart casserole and set aside. In a small saucepan, sauté onion in margarine until tender, but not browned. Remove from heat; stir in garlic powder, bread crumbs, and cheese. Sprinkle on top of corn mixture. Bake uncovered for 1 hour or until browned and set.

Yield: 12 servings

Note: To ripen green tomatoes, place them into a pierced paper bag for several days at room temperature. Do not set tomatoes in the sun to ripen.

Okra Gumbo

6	slices bacon, chopped	1	teaspoon sugar
1	large onion, chopped	1	teaspoon salt
2	pounds fresh okra, sliced	1	teaspoon black pepper
1	(14½ ounce) can diced tomatoes, undrained		

In a heavy skillet over medium-high heat, cook bacon, onion, and okra until lightly browned. Add tomatoes, sugar, salt, and pepper to okra mixture; cover and simmer 20 to 30 minutes or until okra is tender.

Yield: 6 to 8 servings

Note: When buying fresh okra look for firm, brightly colored pods under 4 inches long. Larger pods are tough and fibrous.

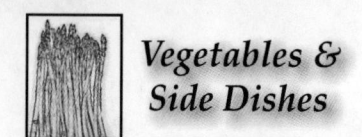

Spinach Casserole

4	(10 ounce) packages frozen chopped spinach	1	(6 ounce) roll jalapeño pepper cheese
½	large onion, chopped fine	½	teaspoon garlic salt
1	stick margarine, divided	½	teaspoon celery salt
2	tablespoons all-purpose flour	1	teaspoon Worcestershire sauce
1	(12 ounce) can evaporated milk	2	cups crushed round buttery crackers

Preheat oven to 350 degrees. Thaw and drain spinach well, gently pressing between layers of paper towels. Set aside. In a large skillet, sauté onion in 4 tablespoons margarine on medium-high heat until tender; add flour; cook, stirring constantly for about 1 minute. Gradually add milk and stir to blend. Add cheese, garlic salt, celery salt, and Worcestershire sauce; stir until cheese melts. Stir in spinach. Spoon into a lightly greased 11 x 7 inch baking dish. Melt the remaining margarine; add crackers and toss to blend; sprinkle over spinach. Bake casserole uncovered for 30 minutes or until bubbly. Let stand 5 minutes before serving.

Yield: 8 to 10 servings

Skillet Summer Squash

2	tablespoons olive oil	½	teaspoon salt
1	small onion, sliced thin	¼	teaspoon freshly ground black pepper
4	medium-size yellow squash, sliced thin	1	bay leaf
½	teaspoon dried basil, crushed		

Heat olive oil in a medium skillet; add onion and sauté until tender, but not browned. Add squash and all remaining ingredients; cook until squash are tender. Remove bay leaf and serve.

Yield: 4 servings

Zucchini with Tomatoes and Herbs

6	medium zucchini, thinly sliced	⅛	teaspoon black pepper
½	cup chopped onion	1	teaspoon dried oregano
2	tablespoons chopped fresh parsley	¼	cup olive oil
1	clove garlic, minced	3	medium tomatoes, peeled and cut into wedges
1	teaspoon salt	½	cup Parmesan cheese

In a large skillet, sauté zucchini, and next 6 ingredients in olive oil until zucchini and onion are tender. Add tomatoes; cook 5 minutes or until thoroughly heated. Spoon into a serving dish and sprinkle with Parmesan cheese. Serve immediately.

Yield: 6 to 8 servings

Note: Zucchini is a popular squash that varies in color from dark to light green. The common market length is 4 to 8 inches. Always select small zucchini because it will be younger, have a thinner skin, and be tender.

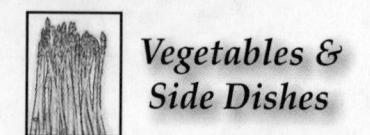

Cheese and Zucchini Casserole

10 small zucchini, sliced	½ teaspoon salt
1 stick margarine	¼ cup chopped fresh chives
¾ cup grated Cheddar cheese	½ teaspoon paprika
¼ cup grated Gruyère cheese	1 cup bread crumbs
1 cup sour cream	¼ cup Parmesan cheese

Preheat oven to 350 degrees. Slice zucchini and simmer in salted water until tender, but still crisp, about 5 minutes; drain thoroughly and spoon into a greased 2½ quart casserole dish. Place margarine and the next 6 ingredients into a covered microwave-safe dish and cook on high power for about 1 minute or until cheeses melt; stir to blend ingredients. Pour cheese mixture over the squash; sprinkle with bread crumbs and Parmesan cheese. Bake for 30 minutes or until bubbly.

Yield: 8 servings

Italian Eggplant

1 large eggplant	1 teaspoon dried basil
1 (14½ ounce) can diced tomatoes, drained	1 teaspoon dried oregano
	½ teaspoon salt
1 medium onion, chopped	½ teaspoon black pepper
1 bell pepper, chopped	½ cup Parmesan cheese
2 tablespoons olive oil	

Peel eggplant and cut into cubes; place into a large mixing bowl. Add tomatoes and the next 7 ingredients; stir to combine ingredients. Spoon mixture into a 1½ quart covered casserole and microwave for 10 minutes on high power; stir. Microwave another 10 minutes or until vegetables are tender. Sprinkle with Parmesan cheese and serve.

Yield: 4 to 6 servings

Note: Although we think of the eggplant as a vegetable, it is actually classified as a fruit. Select eggplants that are firm, smooth-skinned, and heavy for their size.

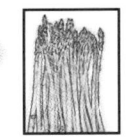

Baked Eggplant

1	large eggplant	1	(10¾ ounce) can mushroom soup, undiluted
1	medium onion, chopped	½	teaspoon Worcestershire sauce
3	tablespoons margarine	1¼	cups crushed round buttery crackers, divided
3	tablespoons chopped fresh parsley		Salt and pepper

Preheat oven to 375 degrees. Cut slice off eggplant lengthwise; cut out pulp, leaving about ¼ inch around sides and bottom of shell. Cook eggplant pulp in salted boiling water until tender; drain well and chop. Sauté onion in margarine until tender; add parsley. Stir in eggplant, soup, Worcestershire sauce, and 1 cup cracker crumbs. Season with salt and pepper. Spoon mixture into eggplant shell and sprinkle with remaining cracker crumbs. Bake for 30 minutes or until browned.

Yield: 4 servings

Eggplant Soufflé

2	medium eggplants, peeled and cubed	½	small bell pepper, finely chopped
1	medium onion, chopped	2	tablespoons olive oil
3	green onions, chopped (white and green parts)	3	eggs, beaten
2	ribs celery, finely chopped	1	cup grated sharp Cheddar cheese
		¼	teaspoon black pepper

Preheat oven to 350 degrees. Cook eggplant in salted boiling water for 20 minutes; drain. In a small skillet, sauté onions, celery, and pepper in olive oil. Combine mixture with eggplant. Add eggs, cheese, and pepper; mix and spoon into a greased 2 quart casserole. Bake uncovered for 35 to 45 minutes or until lightly browned.

Yield: 6 servings

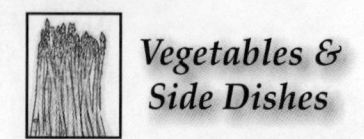
Baked Acorn Squash

2	medium acorn squash	4	tablespoons (½ stick) margarine
½	cup (packed) light brown sugar	1	cup chopped, unpeeled apple Cinnamon

Preheat oven to 350 degrees. Cut acorn squash in half and remove seeds. Place squash, cut side up in a shallow baking dish. Pour ½ inch boiling water into pan. Combine sugar, margarine, and apple; spoon into squash shell. Sprinkle each half with cinnamon. Cover and bake for 1 hour or until tender.

Yield: 4 servings

Note: Acorn squash is a winter squash with a dark green skin and orange flesh. Try this easy method of preparing acorn squash and see if you don't get a thumbs up from your family.

Baked Potato Casserole

6	medium russet potatoes	1	cup grated Cheddar cheese
2	cups sour cream	1	stick margarine
1	bunch green onions, chopped (white and green parts)		Salt and pepper Paprika

Preheat oven to 350 degrees. Cook potatoes in salted boiling water for 30 to 40 minutes or until tender; peel and grate coarsely. Place potatoes into a large bowl; add sour cream, onions, cheese, and margarine; stir to blend. Season with salt and pepper. Spoon mixture into a 13 x 9 inch baking dish and sprinkle with paprika. Bake for 45 minutes.

Yield: 8 servings

Note: There are hundreds of varieties of potatoes grown around the world, but only four basic varieties are grown in America. One of these varieties, the russet, is somewhat dry and mealy after cooking but is excellent for baking, mashing, and frying.

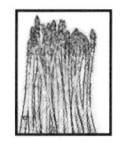
Scalloped Potatoes

6   tablespoons (¾ stick)
    margarine
½   cup chopped onion
⅓   cup all-purpose flour
3   cups milk
2½ cups (10 ounces) grated
    Cheddar cheese, divided

2   teaspoons salt
¼   teaspoon dry mustard
10 cups (2½ pounds) thinly
    sliced potatoes
¼   teaspoon paprika

Preheat oven to 350 degrees. In a medium saucepan melt the margarine; add onion and sauté until soft. Stir in flour and cook over low heat one minute. Gradually add milk, stirring constantly. Cook over medium heat until slightly thickened. Remove from heat; add 1 cup cheese, salt, and mustard; stir until cheese melts. Arrange half the potato slices in a 13 x 9 inch greased baking dish; pour half the sauce over potatoes. Arrange remaining potato slices in dish; add remaining sauce. Cover with foil and bake 1 hour or until potatoes are tender. Uncover, sprinkle with remaining cheese and paprika. Continue baking until cheese is bubbly.

Yield: 10 to 12 servings

Baby Potatoes with Lemon Butter

3   pounds mixed baby potatoes
    (white and red skinned)
6   tablespoons (¾ stick) margarine
6   tablespoons chopped fresh
    parsley, divided

1   tablespoon grated lemon rind
1   tablespoon fresh lemon juice
1½ teaspoons salt
½   teaspoon freshly ground black
    pepper

In a 4 quart stock pot, cook potatoes in salted boiling water for 20 minutes or until tender; drain. Melt margarine in a large, heavy skillet over medium-high heat. Add potatoes, 4 tablespoons parsley, lemon rind, lemon juice, salt, and pepper. Cook until potatoes are heated through and beginning to brown; stir often. Transfer to a 2 quart serving bowl; sprinkle with the remaining parsley and serve.

Yield: 6 to 8 servings

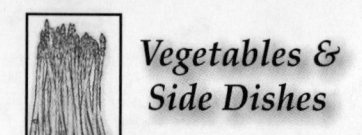

Festive Sweet Potatoes

Potato Mixture

2	(29 ounce) cans sweet potatoes, mashed
1	cup sugar

½	cup milk
1	stick margarine, melted
1	teaspoon vanilla extract
2	eggs, beaten

Streusel Topping

¾	cup coconut
¾	cup (packed) light brown sugar
¼	cup all-purpose flour

4	tablespoons (½ stick) margarine, melted
¾	cup pecans, chopped

Preheat oven to 350 degrees. In a large mixing bowl, mash the sweet potatoes; add sugar and all remaining ingredients; mix well. Spoon potato mixture into a lightly greased 13 x 9 inch casserole dish. In a small bowl, combine all the topping ingredients and mix thoroughly. Sprinkle topping over sweet potatoes and bake uncovered for 30 to 45 minutes or until golden browned.

Yield: 10 to 12 servings

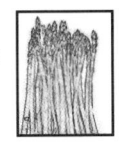

Lemon Sweet Potato Casserole

6 cups (about 3 medium) shredded sweet potatoes	1 cup milk
2 tablespoons margarine, melted	2 eggs, beaten
⅔ cup sugar	½ teaspoon ground cinnamon
	1 (3 ounce) box instant lemon pudding and pie filling

Preheat oven to 325 degrees. Peel and shred potatoes; place into a large bowl; combine with margarine and all remaining ingredients. Spoon mixture into a greased, 2 quart casserole dish. Cover tightly with foil and cook for 1 hour. Remove foil and continue cooking for another 20 to 30 minutes or until top is golden browned.

Yield: 6 servings

Note: Two varieties of sweet potatoes are grown commercially; the pale sweet potato and the dark-skinned variety (often called a "yam"). I prefer the darker skinned variety with its vivid orange sweet flesh and moist texture.

Green Beans with Garlic-Herb Butter

1 pound fresh green beans, trimmed	2 large cloves garlic, minced
4 tablespoons (½ stick) butter	¼ teaspoon chopped fresh or dried rosemary
1 small onion, chopped	¾ teaspoon salt
1 rib celery, chopped	¼ cup chopped fresh parsley

In a large saucepan, add beans to salted boiling water; cover; reduce heat and simmer 10 to 15 minutes or until crisp-tender. Melt butter in a saucepan over medium-high heat; add onion, celery, and garlic. Sauté until tender. Stir in beans, rosemary, salt, and parsley; cook until beans are thoroughly heated. Serve immediately.

Yield: 4 servings

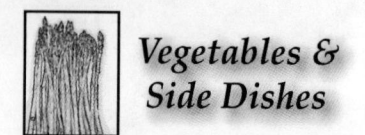

Green Beans and Cabbage

1	(14½ ounce) can green beans	½	teaspoon whole dill seed
½	chicken bouillon cube	¼	teaspoon black pepper
2	tablespoons margarine	1	tablespoon cornstarch
2	tablespoons vinegar	1	tablespoon water
1	tablespoon sugar	1½	cups shredded cabbage

Drain liquid from green beans into a 1½ quart saucepan; set beans aside. Add ½ bouillon cube and the next 5 ingredients to the bean liquid. Heat to boiling. Blend cornstarch and water and add to boiling liquid; stir constantly until mixture thickens and becomes clear. Add cabbage and simmer 5 to 8 minutes or until cabbage is tender. Add green beans and cook until beans are thoroughly heated.

Yield: 6 servings

Brussels Sprouts with Lemon Sauce

3	cups (12 ounces) Brussels sprouts	½	teaspoons grated lemon rind
1	cup chicken broth, divided	1	tablespoon lemon juice
1	teaspoon margarine	⅛	teaspoon black pepper
1	clove garlic, minced	2	teaspoons snipped fresh dill weed (optional)
1½	teaspoons cornstarch		

Trim stems of Brussels sprouts and remove any wilted outer leaves. In a medium saucepan combine Brussels sprouts, ¾ cup broth, margarine, and garlic. Bring to boiling; reduce heat. Cover and simmer for 7 to 10 minutes or until Brussels sprouts are crisp-tender. Transfer sprouts to a serving bowl; keep warm. In a small bowl combine remaining chicken broth, cornstarch, lemon rind, lemon juice, and pepper. Add mixture to hot broth in saucepan. Cook and stir over medium heat until mixture is thickened and bubbly. Stir in fresh dill weed, if desired. Pour lemon sauce over Brussels sprouts and serve.

Yield: 6 servings

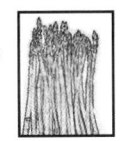

Asparagus with Hollandaise Sauce

Asparagus

1	pound bunch asparagus	¼	cup water
½	teaspoon salt		

Hollandaise Sauce

2	sticks margarine	¼	teaspoon salt
4	egg yolks	⅛	teaspoon cayenne
2	tablespoons lemon juice		

Trim tough portion from asparagus; wash spears and place into a 1½ quart casserole dish with salt and water. Cover and cook in the microwave on high power until crisp-tender, about 2 or 3 minutes. Set aside. To prepare hollandaise sauce, heat margarine in a small saucepan just to bubbling. Place egg yolks, lemon juice, salt, and cayenne into container of an electric blender. Cover and blend on high speed. Immediately remove cover and add margarine in a steady stream. To serve drizzle about 2 tablespoonfuls of sauce over each serving of asparagus.

Yield: 4 servings

Note: This recipe will make about 1¾ cups sauce. Store the unused portion in the refrigerator for later use. The creamy sauce can be used to embellish other vegetables, fish, and egg dishes.

Southwestern Succotash

1 (16 ounce) bag frozen lima
    beans
1 (16 ounce) bag frozen sweet
    white corn
2 tablespoons olive oil
1 tablespoon cumin seeds
1 onion, chopped
2 red bell peppers, chopped
2 poblano chilies, seeded,
    chopped

4 cloves garlic, minced
2 tablespoons chopped fresh
    oregano
1 (14½ ounce) can chicken broth
½ cup heavy cream
⅔ cup chopped fresh cilantro,
    divided
   Salt and pepper

In a 2 quart saucepan, cook lima beans in salted boiling water until just tender, about 6 minutes. Remove from heat. Stir in white corn; drain well. Heat oil in heavy large skillet over medium heat. Add cumin seeds and stir until toasted, about 3 minutes. Add onion and sauté until tender. Add bell peppers, chilies, garlic, and oregano; sauté until peppers are almost tender, about 4 minutes. Stir in lima beans and corn, then broth and cream. Simmer until vegetables are tender and coated with cream, about 30 minutes. Stir in ⅓ cup cilantro. Season with salt and pepper. Transfer to serving bowl; sprinkle with remaining cilantro.

Yield: 10 servings

Note: The poblano chili is dark green with a rich flavor that varies from mild to snappy. They are used in a variety of dishes, but are perhaps best known as the chili of choice for chilies rellenos.

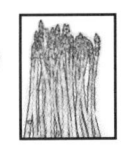

Broccoli and Rice Casserole

1	(10 ounce) package frozen chopped broccoli	1	(10¾ ounce) can cream of chicken soup, undiluted
½	cup chopped onion	1	(6 ounce) jar processed cheese sauce
2	cups instant rice		Salt and pepper
2	cups water		

Preheat oven to 350 degrees. Place broccoli and onion in a microwave-safe casserole. Cover and cook according to directions on broccoli package; drain, and set aside. In a 1½ quart saucepan place rice and water. Bring to boiling and set aside for rice to fluff. Combine broccoli, rice, chicken soup and cheese sauce. Stir to blend. Season with salt and pepper. Spoon mixture into a greased 2 quart casserole. Bake uncovered for 30 minutes or until mixture is completely heated.

Yield: 8 to 10 servings

Cannellini Beans with Bacon and Endive

8	slices bacon, coarsely chopped	2	(15 ounce) cans cannellini beans, drained well
1	medium onion, chopped	⅓	cup canned beef broth
2	large cloves garlic, minced		Salt and pepper
1-1½	pounds curly endive, rinsed, leaves torn coarsely		

Cook bacon in a large heavy pot over medium-high heat until browned and crisp; remove bacon, drain, and set aside. Add onion and garlic to bacon drippings and sauté until soft. Add half of endive and cook until it wilts. Add remaining half of endive; cover and cook until leaves are wilted but still bright green. Add cannellini beans, beef broth, and bacon; cook mixture until heated through, stirring often, about 5 minutes. Season with salt and pepper. Serve.

Yield: 8 servings

Note: The cannellini bean is a white Italian kidney bean, which is available in both dry and canned forms. The use of these beans are particularly popular in soups and salads.

Baked Pork and Beans

4 slices bacon	1 tablespoon Worcestershire sauce
½ cup chopped onion	
2 (15 ounce) cans pork and beans	1 tablespoon prepared yellow mustard
2 tablespoons dark brown sugar	
2 tablespoons catsup	

Preheat oven to 350 degrees. Cook bacon until crisp; drain; crumble and set aside. Drain off all but 2 tablespoons drippings; sauté onion in drippings until soft. Combine onion and next 5 ingredients; stir to blend. Spoon into a lightly greased 1½ quart casserole dish and bake uncovered for 1 hour. Stir beans and sprinkle crumbled bacon on top. Let stand a few minutes before serving.

Yield: 6 servings

Note: This is another all-time favorite. Nothing goes better with a picnic or family outing than grilled hamburgers, baked beans, and coleslaw. Most kids, big and small, will love the tangy flavor of these beans.

Savory Tomato Limas

1 pound dried large lima beans	½ teaspoon salt
3 cups water	½ teaspoon chili powder
1 onion, finely chopped	1 (10¾ ounce) can condensed tomato soup, undiluted
1 clove garlic, minced	
1 tablespoon prepared yellow mustard	2 tablespoons vinegar
	2 tablespoons dark brown sugar
1 tablespoon Worcestershire sauce	¼ pound salt pork, cut into ½ inch cubes

Check beans; rinse and place into a slow cooker with the water. Add onion and all remaining ingredients. Cover and cook on high heat about 5 hours or until beans are tender. Serve.

Yield: 8 to 10 servings

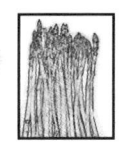

Pinto Beans Seasoned with Salt Pork

1	pound pinto beans		Salt and pepper
2	ounces salt pork	1½	teaspoons ground cumin (optional)
1	medium onion, cut into chunks		
3	cloves garlic, minced	½	teaspoon dried oregano (optional)
2	tablespoon chili powder		

Pick and wash beans; place into a large stock pot. Add 6 to 8 cups hot water and heat beans to boiling for 2 minutes. Remove from heat; let stand for 1 hour. Drain water and add fresh boiling water to cover, 1 inch above beans. Add salt pork, onion, garlic, and chili powder. Cover and simmer for 1½ to 2 hours or until beans begin to soften. Season with salt and pepper; add cumin and oregano, if desired; cook an additional 30 minutes or until beans are soft. Serve.

Yield: 8 to 10 servings

Note: Pinto beans have reddish-brown streaks that turn pink as they soak. Don't add salt until the beans have almost cooked or they will not become tender. If additional water is required during cooking, add hot water. Cold water will cause the beans to split.

Wild Rice and Mushroom Casserole

2	(6 ounce) boxes, wild rice	½	bell pepper, chopped
2	tablespoons margarine	8-10	fresh white mushrooms, sliced
½	bunch green onions, chopped (white and green parts)	½	cup heavy cream
3	ribs celery, chopped	½	cup Parmesan cheese

Preheat oven to 350 degrees. Cook rice according to package directions and set aside. In a small skillet, combine the margarine and the next 4 ingredients; sauté until vegetables are tender. Add vegetables to wild rice; stir to blend. Spoon mixture into a 2 quart greased casserole. Pour cream over rice mixture and sprinkle with cheese. Bake uncovered for 15 minutes or until heated.

Yield: 6 to 8 servings

Note: Wild rice is actually a long-grain marsh grass native to the northern Great Lakes area. Its nutty flavor and chewy texture is especially desirable in dishes such as this one.

Saffron Rice

1	cup long-grain rice, uncooked	2	tablespoons margarine
2	cups chicken broth	⅛	teaspoon powdered saffron
¼	teaspoon salt		

Combine all ingredients in a 1½ quart saucepan. Bring to a boil and stir. Cover, reduce heat and simmer about 15 minutes or until rice is tender and liquid has been absorbed.

Yield: 6 servings

Saffron is the world's most expensive spice. The fragrant spice is the yellow-orange stigmas from the crocus flower. It's expensive because the stigmas are hand picked. It takes about 250,000 to make a pound.

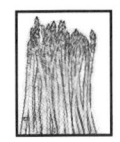

Jean's Quick and Easy
Rice Dressing

2½ cups instant rice	1 medium onion, chopped fine
2½ cups milk	1½ teaspoons garlic salt
3 eggs, beaten	3 tablespoons dried parsley flakes
1½ sticks margarine, melted	
¾ cup processed cheese loaf, cubed	Salt and cayenne

Preheat oven to 350 degrees. In a large bowl mix all ingredients together. Spoon mixture into a 2½ quart covered casserole dish and bake for 1 hour. Stir mixture every 15 minutes.

Yield: 12 servings

Gourmet Macaroni and Cheese

1 (8 ounce) package macaroni	¾ cup water
1 stick margarine	3 drops hot pepper sauce
1 pound sharp Cheddar cheese, grated	2 teaspoons salt
3 eggs, slightly beaten	2 heaping teaspoons dry mustard
1 (12 ounce) can evaporated milk	Parmesan cheese
	Paprika

Preheat oven to 350 degrees. Cook macaroni according to package directions and drain; stir in margarine and cheese; set aside. Combine eggs and the next 5 ingredients; add to macaroni and cheese and blend well. Spoon mixture into a 2½ quart greased baking dish; sprinkle with Parmesan cheese and paprika. Bake for 45 minutes or until lightly browned and bubbly.

Yield: 8 servings

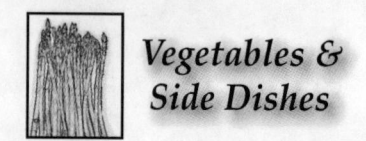

Squash Dressing

1½	pounds yellow squash, sliced	2	(10½ ounce) cans chicken broth
½	cup chopped onion	5	cups corn bread, crumbled
½	cup chopped bell pepper	2	cups milk
½	cup chopped celery	2	eggs, beaten
1	tablespoon margarine	1	teaspoon salt
1	(10¾ ounce) can cream of	¼	teaspoon black pepper
	chicken soup, undiluted	¼	teaspoon poultry seasoning

Preheat oven to 350 degrees. Place squash into a 2 quart saucepan and cover with water; simmer until tender; drain; mash, and set aside. In a small saucepan, combine onion, pepper, celery, and margarine. Sauté on medium-high heat until vegetables are tender, but not browned. In a large bowl, blend chicken soup and chicken broth; stir in sautéed vegetables and corn bread. Add milk and the next 4 ingredients; stir to blend. Add squash and mix well. Spoon mixture into a 13 x 9 inch greased baking dish. Bake uncovered for 30 to 40 minutes or until lightly browned.

Yield: 8 to 10 servings

Note: See recipe for Southern-Style Buttermilk Corn Bread on page 29. This recipe will make enough corn bread for the squash dressing.

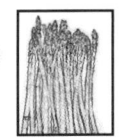

Spinach Dressing

1	pound bacon, diced	1	(14 ounce) can chicken broth
1	pound fresh spinach, washed, sliced into thin strips	2	sticks margarine, softened
		¼	cup finely chopped parsley
8	cups cooked rice, cold	2	cups chopped green onions (white and green parts)
2	(8 ounce) cans mushrooms, stems and pieces, drained	1½	tablespoons dry mustard
4	ribs celery, chopped	1	tablespoon dried chives
2	(8 ounce) cans water chestnuts, drained, sliced		Salt and pepper

Preheat oven to 325 degrees. Fry bacon in a large skillet over medium-high heat until crisp and browned. Remove bacon; drain and set aside. Drain off all but 4 tablespoons of bacon grease from skillet; add spinach and cook until it wilts; remove from heat. Place bacon, spinach and the next 5 ingredients into a large bowl; stir to mix. In a small bowl, combine margarine and the next 4 ingredients; combine mixture with spinach and rice. Season with salt and pepper. Spoon dressing into a greased 13 x 9 inch casserole dish and bake uncovered for 1 hour.

Yield: 10 to 12 servings

Linguine Primavera

1 cup chicken broth	1 medium zucchini, chopped
16 sun-dried tomato halves (not packed in oil)	12 small broccoli florets, separated into bite-size pieces
1 pound linguine	½ cup chopped fresh basil
5 tablespoons olive oil	Salt and pepper
8 cloves garlic, minced	1 cup Parmesan cheese
8 ounces shiitake mushrooms, stemmed, sliced	

Heat broth to a simmer in a small saucepan; remove from heat. Add tomatoes; let stand until soft, about 20 minutes. Drain, reserving broth. Thinly slice tomatoes. Cook linguine in a large pot of salted boiling water until tender, but still firm to bite, stirring occasionally. Heat olive oil in a heavy large skillet over medium-high heat; add garlic and sauté until golden. Add reserved broth, tomatoes, mushrooms, zucchini, broccoli, and basil. Simmer vegetables about 3 minutes or until tender. Drain linguine; return to pot. Add vegetables and toss to combine. Season with salt and pepper. Transfer mixture to bowl; sprinkle with cheese and serve.

Yield: 4 to 6 servings

Orange Glazed Apples

½ cup orange juice	½ cup sugar
2 teaspoons grated orange rind	4 cooking apples

In a heavy skillet, combine orange juice, orange rind, and sugar. Heat mixture just until sugar is dissolved. Remove core from apples and slice each apple into several sections. Place in skillet cut side down. Cover and simmer 10 to 15 minutes or until apples are tender, but still hold their shape. Serve hot or cold.

Yield: 4 to 6 servings

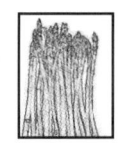

Fettuccine Alfredo

2	(8 ounce) packages fettuccine noodles	1	cup heavy cream
1	stick butter	1	cup Parmesan cheese
			Freshly ground pepper

Cook noodles according to package directions, just until tender. Drain and return to pot. Add butter and cream; mix well. Add Parmesan cheese and toss lightly. Spoon into chafing dish or casserole which can be warmed. Sprinkle individual servings with freshly ground pepper.

Yield: 8 servings

Note: If desired, add fresh sautéed mushrooms to this dish. Sauté 1½ to 2 cups of fresh, thinly sliced white mushrooms in 2 tablespoons of butter until tender. Toss with the fettuccine before adding the Parmesan cheese and freshly ground pepper.

Pineapple Pudding

1	stick margarine, softened	½	cup milk
1¾	cups sugar	½	teaspoon vanilla extract
3	eggs	3	cups (8 to 9 slices) white bread, crust removed, cubed
1	(20 ounce) can crushed pineapple, undrained		

Preheat oven to 325 degrees. In a medium mixing bowl, cream margarine and sugar; add eggs and beat well. Stir in pineapple, milk, and vanilla extract; fold in bread. Pour mixture into a greased 1½ quart casserole; bake uncovered 1 hour or until lightly browned. Serve hot or at room temperature.

Yield: 8 serving

Note: This recipe is best prepared with firm textured bread. If desired, prepare a few hours ahead and refrigerate. Allow time for the casserole dish to warm to room temperature before baking.

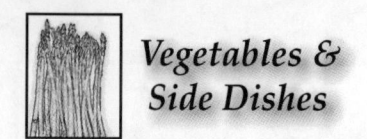

Holiday Cranberries and Apples

Fruit Mixture

2	cups apples, chopped	½	cup sugar
2	cups raw cranberries	⅓	cup (packed) light brown sugar

Topping

1	stick margarine, melted	1	cup quick cooking oats
¼	cup (packed) light brown sugar	⅓	cup chopped pecans
⅓	cup all-purpose flour		

Preheat oven to 350 degrees. In a medium mixing bowl, combine apples, cranberries, and sugars; toss to combine. Spoon mixture into a greased 1½ quart casserole dish. Set aside. Combine the margarine, sugar, and flour; add oatmeal and pecans. Toss mixture together and sprinkle topping over fruit. Bake for 45 minutes or until topping is lightly browned. Serve hot.

Yield: 6 to 8 servings

Baked Fruit Compote

1	(16 ounce) can apricot halves, drained	4	thin orange slices
1	(15.25 ounce) can peach halves, drained	½	cup orange juice
		½	teaspoon grated lemon rind
1	(16 ounce) can whole pitted purple plums, drained	¼	cup (packed) light brown sugar
		2	tablespoons margarine

Preheat oven to 425 degrees. Arrange fruit in a greased 2½ quart casserole dish. Combine orange juice, lemon rind, sugar, and margarine in a small saucepan; heat until sugar is dissolved. Pour over fruit. Bake uncovered for 15 to 20 minutes or until bubbly.

Yield: 10 to 12 servings

Main Dishes

Main Dishes

Beef Tenderloin
with Horseradish Sauce

Beef

1	(3 pound) beef tenderloin	2	tablespoons olive oil
	Salt and freshly ground black pepper		

Sauce

½	cup sour cream	2	green onions, finely chopped (white and green parts)
1	tablespoon prepared horseradish		

Preheat oven to 475 degrees. Sprinkle beef with salt and pepper. In a heavy medium skillet, brown beef in oil on all sides, about 5 minutes. Transfer to a roasting pan and insert a meat thermometer. Place into oven and cook for 10 minutes; reduce oven temperature to 425 degrees and continue cooking for 20 to 25 minutes or until the thermometer reads 145 degrees for medium-rare. Remove tenderloin from the oven and let it stand for 10 minutes before slicing. For the sauce, combine the sour cream, horseradish, and green onions in a small bowl; mix well. Thinly slice the tenderloin and serve with sauce.

Yield: 6 to 8 servings

Note: Tenderloin should not be overcooked. Once removed from the oven, meat will continue to cook slightly. This should be taken into account when determining the doneness.

No Fuss Beef Brisket

1 (7-9 pound) beef brisket, trimmed	1½ teaspoons garlic powder
Salt and pepper	1 cup hickory smoked barbecue sauce

Preheat oven to 500 degrees. Place 2 layers of aluminum foil in a 17 x 11 inch baking pan. Place brisket on foil. Season generously with salt and pepper; sprinkle with garlic powder. Pour barbecue sauce over brisket. Fold over foil and seal tightly. Place into oven and bake for 1 hour. Turn off oven and do not open door until the brisket is cool, about 5 or 6 hours. Remove brisket from sauce. Slice across grain; serve with additional barbecue sauce.

Yield: 12 to 15 servings

Note: Brisket cooked in this manner is always juicy and tender. Reduce cooking time by 10 to 15 minutes for a smaller brisket.

Pepper Steak

1 pound round steak	1 small onion, chopped
Salt and pepper	1 (8 ounce) carton white mushrooms, sliced
¼ teaspoon garlic powder	
1 tablespoon soy sauce	1 tablespoon cornstarch
¼ cup olive oil	1 cup water
1 cup chopped bell pepper	1 cup rice, uncooked
1 cup chopped celery	

Cut steak into serving pieces. In a medium bowl, combine salt, pepper, garlic powder, soy sauce, and olive oil. Add steak and stir to coat with seasonings. In a large skillet, cook meat slowly until tender, about 30 minutes. Add bell pepper, celery, onion, and mushrooms; cook an additional 10 minutes or until tender. Mix cornstarch with water and add to meat and vegetables. Cook until thickened. Cook rice according to directions on package. Serve pepper steak over rice.

Yield: 4 servings

Texas Fried Steak with Country Gravy

Steak

2	pounds round steak, tenderized	1	cup milk
	Salt and pepper		All-purpose flour
1	egg, beaten		Vegetable oil

Country Gravy

4	tablespoons all-purpose flour	Salt and pepper
2	cups milk	

Cut steak into serving portions; season with salt and pepper. Whisk egg and milk together. Dip steak into egg mixture; coat with flour. Allow steak to set for a few minutes and dip again in flour. Shake off excess flour and fry steak in hot oil until golden browned and crisp. Drain on paper towels and keep warm while preparing gravy. Remove all but 4 tablespoons fat from skillet but leave in crusty bits. Add flour; blend and brown on very low heat, using care not to scorch. Remove from heat; add milk. Season with salt and pepper. Return to low heat and simmer until smooth and thickened, stirring constantly. Serve steak with gravy.

Yield: 6 servings

Roast and Gravy

3-4	pounds chuck or shoulder roast	1	(10¾ ounce) can cream of mushroom soup
	Pepper	1	(1 ounce) package dry onion soup mix

Preheat oven to 350 degrees. Place a piece of aluminum foil large enough to completely wrap roast in the center of a 13 x 9 inch casserole dish. Place roast on foil, sprinkle with pepper. Spread undiluted mushroom soup over roast. Sprinkle with dry onion soup mix. Fold foil over and crimp edges to seal securely. Bake 2½ to 3 hours or until roast is tender. Slice roast and serve with gravy.

Yield: 6 to 8 servings

Oriental Beef Stir Fry

2	tablespoons cooking oil	2	bunches green onions, sliced (white and green parts)
1	pound sirloin tip, sliced paper thin across grain	1	(14 ounce) can bean sprouts, drained
3	tablespoons sugar	1	(8 ounce) can water chestnuts, drained, sliced
2	tablespoons all-purpose flour	1	(8 ounce) can sliced mushrooms, undrained
½	cup soy sauce		
⅔	cup water	3	cups cooked rice
1	(8 ounce) can bamboo shoots, drained		Soy sauce (optional)

Heat oil in electric skillet set at 375 degrees. Brown sirloin for 2 to 3 minutes. Combine, sugar, flour, soy sauce, and water. Pour over beef; push to one side. Add bamboo shoots and onions, keeping in separate groups. Continue cooking and tossing each group for 5 to 10 minutes, keeping vegetables separate. Push to side. Add bean sprouts, water chestnuts, and mushrooms, keeping in groups. Cook about 2 minutes until heated through. Serve with hot fluffy rice and additional soy sauce, if desired.

Yield: 4 to 6 servings

Swiss Steak

½	teaspoon salt	¼	cup vegetable oil
½	teaspoon black pepper	1	(14½ ounce) can diced tomatoes
2	pounds round steak (1½ inches thick)	1	large onion, sliced
½	cup all-purpose flour	1	rib celery, chopped

Preheat oven to 300 degrees. Salt and pepper round steak; pound flour into steak. Brown steak in hot oil in a heavy skillet. Add tomatoes, onion, and celery. Cover skillet with aluminum foil and place into oven. Cook for 2 to 2½ hours or until tender; uncover last 30 minutes to cook down sauce. Slice and serve hot.

Yield: 4 to 6 servings

Sweet and Sour Meat Loaf

1	(8 ounce) can tomato sauce	1	egg, beaten
¼	cup (packed) light brown sugar	1	teaspoon salt
¼	cup vinegar	¼	teaspoon black pepper
1	teaspoon prepared yellow mustard	1	small onion, chopped fine
2	pounds lean ground beef	½	cup round buttery crackers, crushed

Preheat oven to 350 degrees. In a small bowl, combine the tomato sauce, sugar, vinegar, and mustard; set aside. In a large bowl, combine the ground beef and the next 5 ingredients. Add ½ of the tomato sauce mixture; blend thoroughly. Shape meat into a loaf and place into a shallow 2 quart baking dish. Pour remaining sauce over meat loaf. Cover and bake for about 1 hour; uncover and bake an additional 15 minutes.

Yield: 8 servings

Quick and Easy Beef Noodle Casserole

1	pound lean ground beef	1	(8½ ounce) can cream-style corn
½	cup chopped onion	1	(2½ ounce) can sliced black olives, drained
1	(10¾ ounce) can tomato soup, undiluted		Salt and pepper
1-2	cans water, divided	1	cup (4 ounces) grated Cheddar cheese
6	ounces egg noodles		

Preheat oven to 350 degrees. In a large skillet cook ground beef until no longer pink; add onion and cook until tender. Stir in the tomato soup, 1 can water, and noodles; cook about 8 to 10 minutes; do not overcook noodles. Add additional water if needed. Add corn and olives; cook until heated, about 3 to 5 minutes. Season with salt and pepper. Spoon ingredients into a greased 2 quart casserole; sprinkle with cheese. Bake uncovered 20 to 30 minutes or until cheese is bubbly.

Yield: 6 to 8 servings

Hamburger Stroganoff

1	pound lean ground beef	1	(10¾ ounce) can cream of
3	slices bacon, diced		mushroom soup, undiluted
1	small onion, chopped	2	teaspoons Worcestershire sauce
¼	teaspoon salt	1	cup sour cream
¼	teaspoon black pepper	6	ounces extra wide noodles
¼	teaspoon paprika	2	tablespoons margarine
			Paprika

In a large skillet, cook ground beef and bacon until meat is no longer pink. Add onion; cook until tender, but not browned. Drain the excess fat; add the salt and the next 4 ingredients. Cook uncovered on low heat, for about 20 minutes, stirring frequently. Stir in sour cream and heat thoroughly; do not boil. Cook noodles according to package directions; drain and toss with margarine. Serve stroganoff over noodles and sprinkle with paprika.

Yield: 4 to 6 servings

Note: This is the first entrée I served my husband. It's still one of his favorite dishes. I usually omit the margarine on the noodles when I am serving this recipe at home.

Western Beef and Bean Dish

1	pound lean ground beef	½	teaspoon garlic powder
1	small onion, chopped fine	1	(1¼ ounce) package taco
1	(23 ounce) can ranch style beans		seasoning mix

In a large skillet, cook beef until no longer pink; add onion and cook until tender; drain excess fat. Add the beans, garlic powder, and taco seasoning mix. Stir to blend. Add enough water to make the desired consistency. Bring to a boil; reduce heat and simmer for about 15 minutes. Serve in bowls with corn bread.

Yield: 6 to 8 servings

Beef and Spaghetti Casserole

1	pound lean ground beef	1	(8 ounce) can mushrooms, stems and pieces, drained
1	bell pepper, chopped	1	(2½ ounce) can sliced olives, drained
1	small onion, chopped		
1	(10¾ ounce) can tomato soup, undiluted	6	ounces spaghetti
1	(8 ounce) can tomato sauce	1	(8 ounce) box processed cheese loaf, grated

Preheat oven to 300 degrees. In a large skillet, cook ground beef until no longer pink; add bell pepper and onion; cook until vegetables are tender. Drain off fat. Add tomato soup, tomato sauce, mushrooms, and olives. Simmer for 15 to 20 minutes. Combine meat mixture with spaghetti cooked according to package directions. Spoon mixture into a greased 2 quart casserole dish and sprinkle with cheese. Bake uncovered 20 to 30 minutes or until cheese is bubbly.

Yield: 8 servings

Note: If you plan to serve this casserole later, prepare meat mixture, cool, and refrigerate. When ready to serve, cook spaghetti and combine with meat mixture. Top with cheese and cook until it is thoroughly heated.

Lazy Lady's Beef and Bean Bake

½	pound lean ground beef	¾	cup (packed) light brown sugar
6	slices bacon, chopped fine	1	(15½ ounce) can kidney beans
½	cup chopped onion	1	(15 ounce) can pork and beans
1	teaspoon prepared yellow mustard	1	(15½ ounce) can white lima beans
2	teaspoons vinegar		

Preheat oven to 300 degrees. In a medium skillet, cook ground beef, bacon, and onion together; drain off excess fat. Combine beef mixture with the remaining ingredients; stir to blend. Spoon mixture into a 2½ quart greased casserole dish. Bake covered for about 1 hour.

Yield: 8 servings

Company Spanish Rice

1	pound lean ground beef	1½	cups rice
¾	cup chopped bell pepper	1	(14½ ounce) can diced tomatoes
1	teaspoon chili powder	1	(6 ounce) can tomato paste
1	teaspoon sugar	2½	teaspoons salt
1	(10½ ounce) can beef bouillon	1	small bay leaf
¼	cup vegetable oil	⅛	teaspoon cayenne
2	cloves garlic, minced	2	cups hot water
¼	cup chopped celery		

Preheat oven to 350 degrees. In a medium saucepan cook ground beef until no longer pink; add bell pepper and cook until tender. Remove from heat; stir in chili powder, sugar, and bouillon. Set aside. In a large skillet, heat the vegetable oil; add garlic and celery; sauté until tender. Add rice and the next 6 ingredients; stir well. Bring to a boil; cover and simmer for about 10 minutes; remove bay leaf. Combine the meat mixture with the rice mixture; stir to blend. Spoon mixture into a greased 3 quart baking dish. Bake for about 30 to 35 minutes. Stir occasionally. Serve hot.

Yield: 8 to 10 servings

Note: This Spanish rice can be served as a main dish, or as a side dish with other Mexican food.

Mexican Mingle

1	pound lean ground beef	1	(10¾ ounce) can cream of chicken soup, undiluted
	Salt and pepper	1	(10 ounce) can enchilada sauce
	Garlic powder		
1	small onion, chopped	1	dozen corn tortillas
1	(4½ ounce) can chopped mild green chilies	2	cups (8 ounces) grated Cheddar cheese
1	(10¾ ounce) can cream of mushroom soup, undiluted		

Preheat oven to 350 degrees. Season ground beef with salt, pepper, and garlic powder. In a large skillet, cook ground beef until it is no longer pink; add onion and cook until tender. Drain fat from meat. Add the green chilies, mushroom soup, chicken soup, and enchilada sauce. Stir and simmer the mixture until well blended. Cut the corn tortillas into quarters. Layer ½ on the bottom of a greased 13 x 9 inch baking dish. Spoon ½ of the meat mixture on top of tortillas; repeat. Sprinkle casserole with grated cheese; bake uncovered until cheese is bubbly.

Yield: 8 to 10 servings

Tex-Mex Enchiladas

1	pound lean ground beef	1	teaspoon paprika
	Salt and pepper	3	cups hot water, divided
1	small onion, chopped	1	dozen corn tortillas
1	(10¾ ounce) can tomato puree	1	(8 ounce) package processed
1	tablespoon chili powder		cheese loaf, grated

Preheat oven to 350 degrees. In a large skillet cook ground beef until no longer pink; season with salt and pepper. Add chopped onion and cook until tender, but not browned; drain fat. Add tomato puree, chili powder, and paprika. Cook for 2 minutes. Remove ½ of the mixture and set aside. Add 1 cup of hot water to mixture remaining in skillet; simmer while preparing enchiladas. Dip each corn tortilla into remaining hot water; place a large spoonful of meat mixture on each tortilla. Sprinkle generously with cheese. Roll up and place seam side down in a greased 13 x 9 inch baking dish. Repeat until all tortillas are filled. Cover rolled enchiladas with remaining meat mixture. Sprinkle remaining cheese on top. Bake uncovered for about 20 to 30 minutes or until bubbly.

Yield: 4 to 6 servings

Note: Chili powder is a blend of dried chilies, red peppers, oregano, cumin, and garlic powder. This pre-mixed blend is thought to be a Texas invention; however, the combination of chile peppers and oregano has been traced to the Aztecs.

Italian Sausage and Pasta Casserole

1	pound bulk Italian sausage	½	cup Parmesan cheese, divided
2	(28 ounce) cans crushed tomatoes	⅛	teaspoon nutmeg
1	bay leaf	2	(10 ounce) packages frozen chopped spinach, thawed and drained
4	cloves garlic, minced		
2	teaspoons sugar	1	(12 ounce) package extra wide noodles, cooked and drained
1	teaspoon dried basil		
½	teaspoon dried oregano	4	green onions, sliced (white and green parts)
½	teaspoon salt		
¼	teaspoon black pepper	1	pound (4 cups) grated mozzarella cheese, divided
4	eggs, beaten		

Preheat oven to 350 degrees. In a 4 quart Dutch oven, cook sausage until no longer pink; drain. Add tomatoes and the next 7 ingredients; bring to a boil. Reduce heat; simmer uncovered, for 1 hour, stirring occasionally. In a large bowl, combine eggs, ¼ cup Parmesan cheese, and nutmeg; mix well. Stir in spinach, noodles, and onions. Remove bay leaf from sauce and discard. Grease two (9 inch) square baking dishes. In each baking dish, layer a fourth of the noodles, then a fourth of the sauce mixture. Top each with 1 cup mozzarella cheese. Repeat layers. Top with remaining Parmesan cheese. Bake uncovered for 30 minutes or until bubbly. Let stand for 10 minutes before serving.

Yield: 8 servings for each casserole

Note: This casserole freezes well. Thaw casserole before baking. Bake at 350 degrees for 1 hour or until heated through. To reduce fat, use Italian turkey sausage packaged as links. Remove the outside casing and cook in the same manner as bulk sausage.

Savory Cabbage Rolls

8	tender cabbage leaves	1	medium onion, finely chopped
¾	pound lean ground beef	2	cloves garlic, minced
½	pound sweet Italian sausage, chopped	1	tablespoon fresh chopped cilantro
2	slices bacon, chopped	1	teaspoon caraway seeds
2	tablespoons grated Cheddar cheese	⅛	teaspoon ground nutmeg
			Salt and pepper
1	egg white	4	teaspoons margarine
2	tablespoons chopped mushrooms	1	(8 ounce) can tomato sauce

Preheat oven to 375 degrees. Cut deeply around the stem of the cabbage to remove the leaves from the core. Blanch leaves in salted boiling water until they are tender, about 2 minutes; drain. Set aside to cool. Combine the ground beef and the next 10 ingredients. Season with salt and pepper; mix thoroughly. Shape into 8 oblong patties. Wrap a cabbage leaf around each patty and secure the roll with a toothpick. Place rolls in a greased 11 x 7 inch baking dish; spread each roll with ½ teaspoon of margarine. Pour tomato sauce over cabbage rolls. Cover and bake for 35 to 40 minutes or until the meat is cooked.

Yield: 4 servings

Moussaka

3	medium onions, sliced	½	teaspoon dried oregano
¾	cup olive oil, divided	2	large eggplants, sliced
1	pound lean ground beef or ground lamb	1	cup milk
			Salt and pepper
1	(8 ounce) can tomato sauce	⅛	teaspoon ground nutmeg
½	teaspoon dried thyme	3	egg yolks

Preheat the oven to 350 degrees. In a medium skillet, sauté the onions in ¼ cup oil until they are transparent; add meat and cook until no longer pink; drain fat. Add the tomato sauce, thyme, and oregano. Stir to blend and simmer. In a medium skillet, heat the remaining ½ cup olive oil and brown the eggplant slices on each side. Drain eggplant slices on paper towels. Grease a 2½ quart baking dish; place a layer of eggplant slices on the bottom of the dish. Spread a layer of the meat mixture over the top; alternate layers of the eggplant and meat until the pan is almost full. In a small saucepan, scald the milk; add salt, pepper, and nutmeg. Beat the egg yolks and gradually add to the scalded milk; cook over medium heat until sauce thickens. Pour this custard-like mixture on top of the casserole and bake for 45 minutes. Cut into squares to serve.

Yield: 4 to 6 servings

Note: Moussaka is a Greek dish characterized by a topping of light custard. Other ingredients such as cheese, artichokes, thinly sliced potatoes, and tomatoes may be added to this dish.

 *Main Dishes*

Spaghetti and Meat Sauce

Meat Sauce

1	large onion, chopped	2	teaspoons dried parsley
4	cloves garlic, minced	1	bay leaf
2	tablespoons olive oil	3	cups water
1	(14½ ounce) can diced tomatoes	2	pounds lean ground beef
2	(8 ounce) cans tomato sauce	1	teaspoon salt
3	(6 ounce) cans tomato paste	½	teaspoon black pepper
1	teaspoon sugar		Parmesan cheese (optional)
1	tablespoon dried oregano		

Spaghetti

1	(12 ounce) package spaghetti	2	teaspoons salt

In a 4 quart stock pot or Dutch oven, sauté onion and garlic in olive oil. Add tomatoes and the next 7 ingredients; simmer 30 minutes. In a large skillet cook ground beef until no longer pink; drain. Season with salt and pepper. Add ground beef to the sauce and simmer for an additional 30 minutes. In a large stock pot, bring 4 quarts of water and salt to a rolling boil. Gradually add spaghetti. Cook 6 to 8 minutes, uncovered, stirring occasionally. Do not overcook. Drain well. Remove ½ of the spaghetti sauce from the stock pot and set aside for later use. Add drained spaghetti to the remaining sauce in the stock pot. Toss lightly to mix. Serve plain or with Parmesan cheese.

Yield: 8 to 10 servings

Note: The meat sauce can be frozen for later use. Also, use this sauce for the lasagna recipe found on page 151.

Lasagna

2   eggs, beaten
1   (15 ounce) container small
       curd cottage cheese
1   (12 ounce) package mozzarella
       or Monterey Jack cheese
1   cup Parmesan cheese, divided

¼   cup chopped fresh parsley
½   recipe (4 cups) meat sauce
1   (8 ounce) package lasagna
       noodles, uncooked
    Pepperoni slices

Preheat oven to 350 degrees. In a medium bowl, combine the eggs, cottage cheese, mozzarella, ½ cup Parmesan cheese, and parsley. Stir to blend and set aside. Lightly grease a 13 x 9 inch baking pan. Pour 1 cup meat sauce on bottom of pan. Layer 3 pieces of uncooked lasagna over sauce; cover with 1 cup sauce. Place ½ of the pepperoni slices on top of sauce and spread ½ of the cheese filling over sauce and pepperoni. Repeat layers of lasagna, sauce, pepperoni and cheese filling. Top with layer of lasagna and remaining sauce. Cover with aluminum foil and bake for 55 to 60 minutes. Remove aluminum foil; bake 10 minutes longer; sprinkle with remaining Parmesan cheese. Allow to stand 10 minutes before cutting into squares for serving.

Yield: 8 to 10 servings

Note: Use the recipe for the meat sauce found on page 150 of this cookbook.

Chicken with Lemon and Garlic Seasonings

4 skinless, boneless chicken breast halves	1 tablespoon olive oil
½ teaspoon salt	4 cloves garlic, minced
½ teaspoon black pepper	1 lemon

Pound chicken breasts with mallet and season with salt and pepper. Heat olive oil in a medium skillet until hot. Add breasts and sprinkle with garlic. Sauté about 7 minutes. Turn chicken breasts, squeeze lemon juice over each and cook an additional 7 minutes or until done.

Yield: 4 servings

Note: After working with uncooked chicken or turkey, you should wash your hands, all surfaces and utensils thoroughly with hot soapy water. Dry your hands with a paper towel.

Patio Broiled Chicken

1 cup vegetable oil	½ teaspoon salt
⅓ cup lemon juice	¼ teaspoon black pepper
3 tablespoons soy sauce	4 broiler-fryer halves (1½ to 2 pounds each)
1 clove garlic, minced	
1 teaspoon dried oregano	

In a medium bowl whisk together all ingredients except chicken. Place chicken in a shallow pan and cover with marinade. Let stand in refrigerator several hours, turning occasionally. Remove from marinade. Place chicken bone side down on grill. Grill over low setting for 15 minutes. Turn chicken and cook with hood down, for approximately 30 to 45 minutes longer, basting occasionally with marinade.

Yield: 4 servings

Chicken Casserole

2	tablespoons margarine	1	(10½ ounce) can onion soup, undiluted
1	cup uncooked long-grain rice	1	(8 ounce) can sliced mushrooms, drained
1	chicken, cut into serving pieces		Paprika
1	(10¾ ounce) can cream of chicken soup, undiluted		

Preheat oven to 325 degrees. Melt margarine in a 13 x 9 inch baking dish. Add uncooked rice. Layer chicken over rice. Mix chicken soup, onion soup, and mushrooms together; pour over the chicken. Sprinkle with paprika. Cover baking dish with aluminum foil. Bake for 1 hour or until chicken is tender.

4 servings

Note: You can vary this recipe by using brown rice in place of white rice, and by substituting fresh sliced mushrooms for canned mushrooms.

Baked Chicken

¼	cup all-purpose flour	4	tablespoons (½ stick) margarine
½	teaspoon salt	1	(10¾ ounce) can cream of chicken soup, undiluted
¼	teaspoon black pepper	1	(4 ounce) can mushrooms, undrained
1	teaspoon paprika	½	cup water
1	(3 pound) chicken, cut into quarters		

Preheat oven to 425 degrees. Combine flour, salt, pepper, and paprika in a 1 gallon size zip-top plastic bag. Add chicken quarters and shake well to coat. Melt margarine in a shallow baking dish which is just large enough to hold the chicken. Arrange chicken in the baking dish, skin side down. Bake, uncovered, for 30 minutes. Remove dish from oven: drain off the fat; turn chicken over. Reduce oven temperature to 375 degrees. In a small saucepan, combine soup, mushrooms, and water; heat and stir until blended. Pour over chicken. Bake an additional 30 to 35 minutes or until chicken is tender. Stir in additional water during baking if more gravy is desired.

Yield: 4 servings

 *Main Dishes*

Chicken with Duck Sauce

1	(8 ounce) jar apricot preserves	1	(1 ounce) envelope onion soup mix	
1	(8 ounce) bottle Russian dressing	6	large chicken breasts	

Preheat oven to 300 degrees. In a small bowl, mix apricot preserves, dressing, and soup mix. Place the chicken breasts in a greased 13 x 9 inch baking dish and spread apricot mixture over the chicken. Bake uncovered for about 2 hours.

Yield: 6 servings

Baked Rosemary and Garlic Chicken

1	(3-4 pound) roaster chicken	½	teaspoon black pepper
1	clove garlic, minced	4	sprigs fresh rosemary
1	lemon, juiced, and zest removed	2	tablespoons olive oil Paprika
1	teaspoon salt		

Preheat oven to 375 degrees. Rinse chicken and pat dry. In a small bowl, mix garlic, lemon juice, salt, and pepper; rub under skin of breast and thigh area. Place sprigs of rosemary in cavity of chicken; tie legs up with string. Mix lemon zest and olive oil together and spread over chicken skin. Sprinkle generously with paprika. Place chicken on rack in a large baking dish, breast side up; cover and bake 25 to 30 minutes per pound or until very tender. Let stand 10 minutes before cutting. Remove rosemary from cavity and discard. Slice chicken and serve.

Yield: 6 servings

Note: This is an easy way to roast a chicken. A good variation is to substitute onion, orange, and basil leaves for the garlic, lemon, and rosemary. The basil leaves can be slipped under the skin with the orange and thinly sliced onion. Both variations of this recipe are delicious.

Chicken Fricassee

4	skinless boneless chicken breast halves	2	teaspoons dried marjoram
	Salt and pepper	¼	teaspoon ground nutmeg
1	(10½ ounce) can low-salt chicken broth	⅔	cup heavy cream
2	cups green onions, chopped, divided (white and green parts)	2	tablespoons all-purpose flour
			Buttered noodles (optional)

Season chicken with salt and pepper; place in a medium skillet. Add chicken broth, 1½ cups onions, marjoram, and nutmeg. Bring broth to boil. Reduce heat to low, partially cover skillet and simmer until chicken is just cooked through, about 10 to 12 minutes. Using tongs, transfer chicken to plate. Whisk cream and flour together in a small bowl. Gradually whisk mixture into simmering broth. Stir until broth thickens to sauce consistency and coats spoon, about 3 minutes. Return chicken to sauce. Simmer until heated through, about 1 minute. To serve, spoon sauce over chicken; sprinkle with remaining green onions.

Yield: 4 servings

Note: This easy and delicious recipe can be doubled, if desired. It is especially flavorful when served over buttered noodles.

Baked Chicken
with Barbecue Sauce

1	(3½-4 pound) chicken, cut into serving pieces	1½	teaspoons Worcestershire sauce
1	(14½ ounce) can crushed tomatoes with added puree	1	teaspoon salt
		½	teaspoon black pepper
¼	cup (packed) light brown sugar	½	teaspoon dried thyme
3	tablespoons apple cider vinegar	¼	cup prepared yellow mustard

Preheat oven to 350 degree. Place chicken in a 13 x 9 inch glass baking dish. Whisk together all the remaining ingredients in a small saucepan except the mustard; heat to boiling. Remove from heat; whisk in mustard. Pour sauce evenly over chicken. Cover baking dish with aluminum foil and bake for about 1 hour. Uncover; turn and baste chicken; cook another 30 minutes or until tender, browned, and glazed.

Yield: 6 servings

Baked Chicken Salad

2	cups cooked, chopped, chicken	2	tablespoons lemon juice
2	cups chopped celery	½	cup sliced almonds
½	cup chopped bell pepper	½	(10¾ ounce) can cream of chicken soup, undiluted
2	tablespoons grated onion		Salt and pepper (optional)
1	(2 ounce) jar chopped pimientos, drained	3	cups crushed potato chips
½	cup mayonnaise	½	cup grated Cheddar cheese

Preheat oven to 350 degrees. In a large bowl, combine chicken and the next 8 ingredients. Season with salt and pepper. Lightly toss the ingredients and spoon mixture into a 1½ quart greased casserole. Sprinkle top with potato chips and Cheddar cheese. Bake uncovered for 30 minutes or until heated through and lightly browned.

Yield: 6 servings

Hungarian Chicken Paprika

1	cup chopped onions	1	(2-3 pound) chicken
2	tablespoons vegetable oil	3	tablespoons all-purpose flour
1	teaspoon salt	1	(8 ounce) carton sour cream
2	tablespoons paprika	1	(12 ounce) package extra wide
2	chicken bouillon cubes		egg noodles

In a large stock pot, sauté onions in vegetable oil until tender. Add salt, paprika, bouillon cubes, and enough water to cover chicken. Bring the water to boiling; boil until cubes are dissolved. Add chicken, cover and cook until tender. Remove chicken from broth; cool; remove bones and set aside. Blend the flour with a small amount of the broth; add slowly to the broth in the pot and whisk; cook until thickened. Stir a small amount of the thickened sauce into the sour cream; whisk sour cream into the thickened sauce. Add the boned chicken and heat thoroughly. Do not boil. Cook the noodles according to package directions. Serve chicken over the noodles.

Yield: 8 servings

Note: Paprika is the ground spice of dried capsicum peppers (sweet red peppers). It can be purchased in sweet, moderately hot and hot. Select Hungarian paprika for the best flavor.

Chicken Spaghetti

4	large chicken breasts
1	teaspoon salt
1	large onion, chopped
1	cup chopped celery
1	bell pepper, chopped
1	(4 ounce) jar diced pimientos, drained

1	(8 ounce) can sliced mushrooms, drained
1	(10¾ ounce) can cream of mushroom soup, undiluted
1	(8 ounce) package spaghetti, cooked
1	(16 ounce) package (4 cups) Cheddar cheese, grated, divided

Preheat oven to 350 degrees. Place chicken into a large stock pot; add salt and enough water to cover chicken. Cook chicken until tender; remove from broth and cool. Cut chicken into bite-size pieces and set aside. Combine onion, celery, pepper and ¼ cup of the chicken broth; cover and cook in a microwave oven on high power about 15 minutes or until vegetables are tender. In a large bowl, combine the chicken and all remaining ingredients except 1 cup of cheese; stir to blend. Place chicken mixture into a greased, 13 x 9 inch baking dish. Sprinkle top with remaining cheese. Bake uncovered for 20 to 30 minutes, or until heated through and the cheese is bubbly.

Yield: 10 to 12 servings

Chicken Lasagna Casserole

1 cup milk	⅓ cup chopped bell pepper
1 (10¾ ounce) can cream of mushroom soup, undiluted	⅓ cup chopped onion
½ teaspoon poultry seasoning	¼ cup chopped fresh parsley
2 (3 ounce) packages cream cheese, softened	1 (8 ounce) package lasagna noodles, cooked and drained
1 cup small curd cottage cheese	3 cups cooked, diced chicken
⅓ cup sliced, stuffed green olives	1½ cups bread crumbs
	2 tablespoons margarine, melted

Preheat oven to 350 degrees. Heat together in a small saucepan, the milk, mushroom soup, and poultry seasoning; stir to blend and set aside. In a medium bowl, beat together the cream cheese and cottage cheese; stir in the olives, bell pepper, onion, and parsley. Place a thin layer of the soup mixture on the bottom of a greased 13 x 9 inch baking dish. Layer ½ of the lasagna noodles; spread with half the cheese mixture, half the chicken, and half of the remaining soup mixture. Repeat the layers. Toss the bread crumbs with the margarine and place on top of the casserole. Bake for 30 minutes or until heated through and bubbly.

Yield: 8 to 10 servings

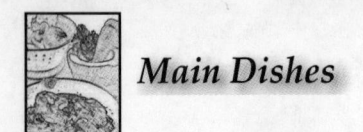

Baked Chicken Casserole

2	cups chopped celery		1	cup mayonnaise
½	cup chopped onion		1	(8 ounce) can water chestnuts, drained, sliced
4	tablespoons (½ stick) margarine, divided		½	cup sliced almonds
3	cups cooked, diced, chicken		1	cup bread crumbs
2	cups cooked rice			

Preheat oven to 350 degrees. In a small saucepan, sauté the celery and onion in 2 tablespoons of margarine until tender, but not browned. Place the celery and onion into a large mixing bowl; add chicken and the next 4 ingredients. Toss the mixture together and spoon into a greased 13 x 9 inch baking dish. Combine the remaining margarine and bread crumbs in a small bowl; sprinkle on top of the casserole. Bake uncovered for 45 minutes or until casserole is heated through.

Yield: 10 to 12 servings

Note: Add a tablespoon of oil to the water when cooking rice to keep the grains separated. Simmer in a large heavy pan so the rice at the bottom doesn't scorch or boil over. Don't stir simmering rice because it mashes the grains and makes the rice gummy.

Chicken-Vegetable Pie

Chicken Mixture

1	(4-5 pound) chicken, cut up
2½	quarts water
2	teaspoons salt
1	clove garlic, crushed
4	peppercorns
1	rib celery with leaves, coarsely chopped
1	large onion studded with 4 whole cloves
3	carrots, cut into 1-inch pieces
12	small white onions
4	large fresh white mushrooms
6	tablespoons (¾ stick) margarine
⅔	cup all-purpose flour
	Salt and pepper
½	cup cooked or canned sweet peas
1	tablespoon chopped fresh parsley

Pie Crust

1½	cups all-purpose flour
1	stick margarine, softened
1	egg yolk
1	teaspoon ice water
1	tablespoon milk

Place chicken into a large stock pot, cover with water; add salt, garlic, peppercorns, celery, and onion studded with cloves. Simmer about 1½ hours, or until tender. Remove chicken from broth; cool; remove skin and bones; chop. Set chicken aside. Discard vegetables and skim fat from broth. Add carrots, onions, and mushrooms to broth. Cook 15 minutes; remove mushrooms; continue cooking carrots and onions until tender. Slice mushrooms and set aside. Remove carrots and onions from broth and place with mushrooms; strain broth and measure 4 cups. Refrigerate remaining broth for another use. Melt margarine in a large skillet; add flour and cook about 3 minutes. Gradually stir in the 4 cups broth. Cook until sauce thickens. Season with salt and pepper. Pour half of sauce into bottom of a greased 3 quart oval baking dish. Arrange chicken, carrots, onions, and mushrooms over the sauce. Sprinkle with peas and parsley; pour in remaining sauce. Set aside. Place flour into a small bowl; cut in the margarine. Add egg yolk and ice water; blend well. Form into a ball and roll out to fit top of casserole between two sheets of wax paper. Fit pastry over casserole; turn edge under; press pastry against side of dish with fork to seal. Cut steam vents in pastry and brush top with milk. Bake at 400 degrees for 45 minutes or until crust is golden browned and filling is bubbly.

Yield: 6 servings

Country-Style
Chicken and Dumplings

1	(3½-4 pound) chicken, cut up	2	cups all-purpose flour
2	quarts water	1	teaspoon baking powder
1½	teaspoons salt	½	teaspoon salt
½	teaspoon black pepper	2	tablespoons shortening
1	carrot, cut in half	½-¾	cup cold water
1	rib celery, cut in half	1	cup milk, heated
1	medium onion, quartered		Flour (optional)

Place chicken into a large stock pot; cover with water; add salt and the next 4 ingredients. Simmer chicken and vegetables for about 1 hour or until tender. Remove chicken; cool; remove skin and bones and coarsely chop; set aside. Discard vegetables and skim fat from broth. Strain broth if desired. Allow broth to simmer while preparing the dumplings. Combine flour, baking powder, and salt; cut in shortening until mixture is crumbly. Add cold water and stir until ingredients are moistened. Knead on lightly floured board about 30 seconds. Roll dough to ⅛ inch thickness; cut into (1 x 3 inch) strips. Bring simmering broth to a boil and drop dumplings into broth, one at a time. Cover, reduce heat and simmer 20 to 30 minutes or until dumplings are tender. Heat milk and add to dumplings. Add chicken and heat thoroughly. If liquid is too thin for dumplings, mix a little flour with water and add slowly to the broth to thicken.

Yield: 6 servings

Chicken and Dressing Casserole

4	large chicken breasts	1	(10¾ ounce) can cream of mushroom soup, undiluted
1	teaspoon salt	1	(8 ounce) package herb-seasoned stuffing mix
1	(10¾ ounce) can cream of chicken soup, undiluted	1	stick margarine, melted

Place chicken into a large stock pot with enough water to cover chicken; add salt. Bring to a boil; reduce temperature and simmer for about 1 hour until chicken is tender. Remove chicken from broth. Strain broth, reserving 2⅔ cups. Bone chicken; cut meat into small pieces; set aside. Combine soups and the 2⅔ cup chicken broth; whisk to blend; set aside. Combine the stuffing mix and margarine; reserve ¼ cup for topping. Spoon half of the stuffing mixture into a lightly greased 13 x 9 inch baking dish; place ½ of the chicken on top of stuffing; cover with ½ of the soup mixture. Repeat layers and top casserole with the reserved stuffing mix. Cover and refrigerate overnight. Remove casserole from refrigerator 15 minutes before baking. Bake uncovered in a preheated 350 degree oven for 45 minutes or until casserole is heated through.

Yield: 8 to 10 servings

Chicken with Rice Dressing

2 tablespoons margarine, melted	1 (14½ ounce) can chicken broth
1 tablespoon lemon juice	½ cup water
1 (3-4 pound) chicken, cut up	¼ pound bulk pork sausage
Salt and pepper	¾ cup chopped green onions (white and green parts)
1½ cups uncooked instant rice	1 cup chopped celery

Preheat oven to 400 degrees. Combine margarine and lemon juice; brush chicken with mixture; season with salt and pepper. Place chicken into a 13 x 9 inch baking dish; bake for 30 minutes. Combine rice, chicken broth, and water in a medium saucepan; bring to a boil. Reduce heat; cover and simmer about 5 minutes or until all broth is absorbed. Set aside. Cook sausage, onions, and celery in a medium skillet until sausage is no longer pink. Combine rice and sausage mixture. Spoon mixture around chicken; bake for an additional 30 minutes.

Yield: 6 servings

Chicken with Mexican Corn Bread Dressing

2 (6 ounce) packages cornbread mix (1 Mexican, 1 plain)	2 (10¾ ounce) cans cream of chicken soup, undiluted
½ large onion, chopped	3 cups chicken broth
½ cup chopped bell pepper	Salt and pepper
2 ribs celery, chopped	1 (3½-4 pound) chicken, cooked and boned
3 tablespoons margarine	

Bake the cornbread as directed; cool, crumble and set aside. In a medium skillet, sauté the onion, pepper, and celery in margarine until tender, but not browned. Add vegetables, chicken soup, and chicken broth to the corn bread; stir to blend. Season with salt and pepper. Place ½ of the dressing into a greased 13 x 9 inch baking dish; place chicken on top of dressing; add remaining dressing. Bake uncovered in a preheated 350 degree oven for 30 minutes or until bubbly.

Yield: 8 to 10 servings

Orange-Glazed
Roasted Chicken with Wild Rice

Roast Chicken

1	large shallot, minced	½	teaspoon salt
1	tablespoon vegetable oil	¼	teaspoon ground marjoram
1	(12 ounce) can orange juice concentrate	1	teaspoon rubbed sage
1½	cups water	½	teaspoon black pepper
2	tablespoons honey	1	(4-5 pound) whole chicken

Wild Rice

2	(6 ounce) packages long-grain and wild rice mix	2	cloves garlic, minced
1	medium onion, chopped	½	cup sweetened dried cranberries, chopped
2	ribs celery, chopped	1	teaspoon rubbed sage
1	fennel bulb, chopped	¼	teaspoon black pepper
1	tablespoon vegetable oil		

Preheat oven to 350 degrees. In a medium skillet, sauté shallot in vegetable oil over medium-high heat for about 3 minutes or until tender. Add orange juice concentrate and the next 6 ingredients; whisk until blended. Place chicken, breast side up, on a rack in an aluminum foil-lined roasting pan. Drizzle with juice mixture. Bake for about 2 hours and 15 minutes or until chicken is tender. Baste chicken about every 30 minutes and loosely cover with aluminum foil after about 30 minutes, if necessary. While chicken is baking, cook rice according to package direction, omitting fat. In a large skillet, sauté onion, celery, and fennel in oil for about 5 to 7 minutes. Add garlic and continue to sauté another 2 minutes. Combine onion mixture, rice, cranberries, sage, and pepper; stir to blend. Serve with chicken and extra sauce.

Yield: 8 servings

Note: Sage is a native Mediterranean herb with a slightly bitter, musty mint taste, and pungent aroma. It is available fresh and dried. Dried sage comes whole, rubbed (crumbled), and ground.

Baked Cornish Hens with Rice Dressing

Cornish Hens

4	Cornish hens
	Salt and pepper
4	tablespoons (½ stick) margarine, melted

3	tablespoons dried rosemary
3	tablespoons dried thyme

Rice Dressing

1	cup long-grain white rice
1	quart water
2	teaspoons salt, divided
¼	pound ground lamb
1	large onion, chopped fine
3	tablespoons pine nuts

¼	cup whole blanched almonds
4	tablespoons (½ stick) margarine, divided
¼	teaspoon black pepper
½	teaspoon ground allspice
½	teaspoon ground cardamom

Preheat oven to 350 degrees. Rinse hens and pat dry. Sprinkle cavity with salt and pepper. Brush outside with melted margarine and rub rosemary and thyme all over the hens. Tuck under wings; tie legs together; place breast side up on rack in a roasting pan. Bake uncovered 1 hour or until juices run clear. If hens begin to brown too much, tent with aluminum foil after about 30 minutes. Start preparing the dressing after hens are placed into the oven. Cover rice with cold water; let stand 10 minutes; drain. In a large saucepan, bring 1 quart water to boiling; add 1 teaspoon salt and the rice. Simmer uncovered, 5 minutes (rice will be partially cooked). Drain rice and toss with lamb and onion; set aside. In a large skillet, sauté pine nuts and almonds in 2 tablespoons margarine until golden. Remove with slotted spoon; set aside. Add remaining 2 tablespoons margarine to skillet. Add rice mixture; sauté until golden browned about 10 minutes. Stir in the pine nuts, almonds, remaining 1 teaspoon salt, the pepper, allspice, and cardamom; toss lightly to combine. Place dressing into a greased 2 quart casserole; bake uncovered about 30 minutes. Serve with hens.

Yield: 4 servings

Note: Since Cornish hens are so small the relative amount of meat to bone is small. One hen is usually considered a single serving. They are delicious roasted and make an elegant dish served with the rice dressing.

Roast Turkey

1	(20-24 pound) turkey, thawed
1	small orange, halved
6	tablespoons (¾ stick) butter, softened

Giblet gravy (optional)
Corn bread dressing (optional)

Preheat oven to 350 degrees. Remove giblets from cavity; reserve for gravy. Wash the turkey inside and out with cold water. Pat dry with paper towels. Squeeze the orange inside the cavity and over the outside of the bird to freshen it. Close the turkey with poultry lacers; tie the legs together; tuck the wing tips under the back of the bird. Rub the turkey all over with the softened butter. Line a large, deep roasting pan with two generous lengths of aluminum foil, making a cross shape in the bottom of the pan. Place a rack in the pan, on top of the foil. Lay the turkey in the roasting pan on the rack, breast-side up. Close foil, crimping the top part over the breast. Roast for about 3 hours covered; uncover and roast an additional 1½ to 2 hours uncovered, basting the turkey often with the pan juices to brown the bird. The turkey is ready when the legs move easily in the sockets and the internal temperature reads 180 degrees Fahrenheit on a meat thermometer inserted into the thickest part of the thigh. Allow turkey to cool 15 to 20 minutes before carving. Serve with giblet gravy and corn bread dressing.

Yield: 12 or more servings

Note: Recipes for Giblet Gravy and Corn Bread Dressing are found on page 168.

Giblet Gravy

	Giblets and neck from turkey	⅛	teaspoon black pepper
1	onion, chopped	4	cups water
2	ribs celery with leaves	⅓	cup turkey drippings, strained
1	carrot, cut in chunks	⅓	cup all-purpose flour
1	teaspoon salt		

Place giblets and neck from turkey into a medium saucepan; add onion and the next 5 ingredients. Simmer until giblets are tender. Remove giblets and chop fine. Strain broth and set aside 2 cups for gravy. To make gravy, blend turkey drippings and flour together; whisk in the broth. Cook over medium heat until thickened; add giblets and continue to cook until mixture is thoroughly heated. Serve with turkey and dressing.

Yield: 3 cups gravy

Corn Bread Dressing

6	cups corn bread	1	stick margarine, melted
4	cups white bread	4	eggs, beaten
4	cups chicken broth	2	teaspoons salt
1½	cups chopped onions	1	teaspoon black pepper
1	cup chopped celery	1	teaspoon poultry seasoning

Preheat oven to 350 degrees. Crumble corn bread and tear white bread into small pieces; place into a large mixing bowl. Pour broth over breads and soak. Sauté the onions and celery in margarine until tender; combine with the breads. Add eggs and seasonings. Mix thoroughly. Spoon mixture into a greased 4 quart or larger baking dish. Bake uncovered for 1 hour or until lightly browned.

Yield: 12 to 15 servings

Note: Use the recipe for Southern Buttermilk Corn Bread found on page 29, or prepare corn bread using 2 (6 ounce) packages of corn bread mix. This is a delicious and moist dressing. It can be frozen, thawed, and reheated when needed.

Baked Ham Supreme
with Orange Pineapple Sauce

Baked Ham

1	(12-15 pound) ham
1	cup (packed) light brown sugar

1	teaspoon dry mustard
2	tablespoons vinegar
	Whole cloves (optional)

Sauce

1	cup sugar
¼	teaspoon salt
2	tablespoons cornstarch
1	tablespoon all-purpose flour
1	(8 ounce) can crushed pineapple, drained, reserve juice

1¼	cups orange juice
¼	cup lemon juice
1	tablespoon margarine

Preheat oven to 325 degrees. Remove wrap from ham; rinse thoroughly and pat dry with paper towels. Place ham into a large roasting pan on a rack. Roast approximately 16 to 17 minutes per pound or about 3 hours and 15 minutes for a 12 pound ham. About 45 minutes before ham is finished baking, remove from oven. Remove rind; score the fat by cutting about ¼ inch into fat surface into squares or diamonds. Mix brown sugar, mustard, and vinegar; spread on ham. Stud each square with whole cloves, if desired. Return to oven and finish baking. Allow to cool slightly before slicing. Prepare sauce while ham is baking. In a medium saucepan, combine sugar, salt, cornstarch and flour; blend. Drain the pineapple and set aside. Add enough water with pineapple juice to make ½ cup liquid. Combine the pineapple, orange and lemon juices; gradually add to dry ingredients. Cook over low heat, stirring until it boils and thickens, about 3 minutes. Remove from heat; add crushed pineapple and margarine; stir to blend. Serve with ham.

Yield: 12 or more servings ham, 4 cups sauce

Pork Chops and Rice Casserole

1	cup long-grain white rice, uncooked	1	can water
1	(10½ ounce) can beef consommé	6	large pork chops
			Salt and pepper
		2	tablespoons vegetable oil

Preheat oven to 350 degrees. Lightly grease a 13 x 9 inch baking dish; place 1 cup of rice on bottom of dish; add beef consommé and water. Set aside. Lightly season pork chops with salt and pepper. In a large skillet brown chops in vegetable oil. Place pork chops on top of rice. Cover baking dish with aluminum foil and bake for about 1 hour or until rice has absorbed all the liquid.

Yield: 6 servings

Note: To save time, this casserole can be prepared without browning the pork chops. Although it is delicious either way, I prefer to brown the chops.

Gourmet Baked Pork Chops with Herb Stuffing

6	(1 inch thick) pork chops	2	cups herb-seasoned stuffing mix
4	tablespoons (½ stick) margarine		
1	medium onion, chopped fine	1	tablespoon chopped fresh parsley
1	(4½ ounce) jar mushrooms, drained, chopped fine	4-6	tablespoons sour cream

Preheat oven to 350 degrees. Slice pockets in each pork chop; set aside. Melt margarine in a medium skillet; add onion and sauté until tender; add mushrooms and cook 2 minutes. Stir in stuffing mix and parsley; toss ingredients together. Add sour cream and stir to blend. Place equal portions of stuffing into pork chops. Secure with a wooden toothpick. Arrange pork chops in a 13 x 9 inch baking pan. Add a small amount of water. Cover pan and bake for 30 minutes; remove cover and bake an additional 30 minutes. Serve immediately.

Yield: 6 servings

Grilled Pork Chops

½ cup fresh orange juice
¼ cup olive oil
1 clove garlic, minced
2 teaspoons ground cumin
½ teaspoon ground cinnamon

Salt and freshly ground black pepper
8 (¾-1 inch thick) boneless center-cut pork chops

In a large bowl, combine the orange juice, and the next 5 ingredients; whisk to blend. Add the pork chops and coat well. Cover and refrigerate overnight. Remove from the refrigerator 1 hour before grilling. Place the chops on a clean grill; cook for about 8 minutes on each side, brushing with marinade. Serve hot.

Yield: 8 servings

Note: Pork is now bred very lean and cooks quickly. Do not cook pork too long or you'll risk drying out the meat.

Sauerkraut and Ribs

2 pounds, spareribs
Vegetable oil
Salt and pepper

1 (20 ounce) can sauerkraut, drained

Cut spareribs into 3 or 4-rib pieces. Brown ribs in a small amount of oil in a large skillet. Season with salt and pepper. Place sauerkraut into a 2 to 3 quart saucepan. Arrange ribs on top of sauerkraut; add enough water to cover sauerkraut. Simmer for about 1 hour or until ribs are tender. Drain liquid and serve spareribs by arranging on top of sauerkraut.

Yield: 4 servings

Sweet and Sour Pork

4	pounds pork	½	cup vinegar
	Salt and pepper	¼	cup soy sauce
1	large onion, sliced	2	(20 ounce) cans pineapple
½	cup (packed) light brown sugar		chunks, drained, reserve juice
½	cup cornstarch	2	bell peppers, sliced

Preheat oven to 350 degrees. Cut pork into (1½ inch) cubes; season with salt and pepper. Place pork into a large baking dish and add onions. Bake for 1 hour, or until tender; turning twice. In a 2 quart saucepan combine the brown sugar and cornstarch. Stir in the vinegar, soy sauce and pineapple juice, plus enough water to make 2½ cups of liquid. Cook slowly until thickened and clear. Add the bell peppers and cook about 3 minutes. Add the pineapple chunks and heat thoroughly. Drain the pork; place into a 4 quart casserole and add sauce. Serve immediately.

Yield: 8 servings

Barbecue Ribs

3-4	pounds spareribs	1	onion, sliced
½	teaspoon salt	1	(16 ounce) bottle barbecue
½	teaspoon black pepper		sauce

Preheat oven to 500 degrees. Cut the spareribs into 3 or 4-rib pieces; season with salt and pepper. Place ribs in a broiler pan and broil for about 15 minutes or until browned. Remove from oven and place into a large crock pot; add onion and cover with barbecue sauce. Cover; cook on low 8 to 10 hours or high 4 to 5 hours.

Yield: 6 servings

Note: This is an easy way to cook ribs. The meat falls off the bones after hours of slow cooking and is tender and juicy.

Pork Loin Roast

2	tablespoons olive oil		2	teaspoons minced fresh rosemary
1	tablespoon margarine, melted		1	(4 pound) center loin (rib) roast
6	cloves garlic, minced			Salt and pepper
1	tablespoon minced fresh sage			

Preheat oven to 350 degrees. Whisk olive oil and the next 4 ingredients together in a small bowl to blend. Place pork in a large roasting pan. Season with salt and pepper. Rub herb mixture over pork. Cover pork loosely with aluminum foil and roast 2½ to 3 hours or until internal temperature reaches 185 degrees Fahrenheit.

Yield: 6 servings

Pork Tenderloin Medallions

2	tablespoons olive oil		Salt and freshly ground pepper
½	cup finely diced shallots	¼	cup low sodium chicken broth
1½	pounds pork tenderloin, thinly sliced	1	teaspoon margarine

Heat the oil in a large skillet and add the shallots. Sauté over medium heat; add the pork and sprinkle lightly with salt and pepper. Sauté for 3 to 4 minutes or until juices are clear, not pink, turning frequently. Remove the tenderloin medallions to a serving platter and keep warm. Add the chicken broth to the skillet and bring to a boil. Stir until the sauce has reduced by about half, then stir in the margarine. Pour over the pork and serve immediately.

Yield: 6 servings

Sausage and Macaroni Casserole

1	pound bulk sausage, hot or mild	½	teaspoon salt
1	(14½ ounce) can diced tomatoes, undrained	¼	teaspoon black pepper
		½	teaspoon chili powder
1	large bell pepper, thinly sliced	3	cups macaroni, cooked
1	large onion, chopped	1½	cups sour cream
			Round buttery cracker crumbs

Preheat oven to 350 degrees. In a large skillet, cook sausage until browned; drain well. Discard fat from sausage; return sausage to skillet; stir in tomatoes and the next 5 ingredients. Cover and cook over medium heat about 10 minutes, stirring occasionally. Add cooked macaroni and sour cream. Stir to blend. Spoon mixture into a greased 3 quart casserole. Sprinkle cracker crumbs on top. Bake uncovered until hot and bubbly, about 20 minutes.

Yield: 6 servings

Fried Fish Fillets

2	pounds or more fish fillets	1	cup cornmeal
¼-½	cup prepared yellow mustard	⅔	cup fish fry mix
	Salt and pepper	⅓	cup cornstarch
	Garlic powder		Vegetable oil

In a large bowl toss the fillets with the mustard to generously coat the fish. Season fish with salt, pepper, and garlic powder. Mix the cornmeal, fish fry mix, and cornstarch together in a large bowl. Add the fish and toss to coat. In a large heavy skillet, fry the fish fillets in medium-hot oil until golden browned. Serve immediately.

Yield: 4 servings

Note: Make sure the oil is hot enough for frying before you add fish to the skillet, otherwise the fish will absorb the oil and be soggy. Cornstarch keeps the coating on the fish as it fries and results in crispy fillets.

Baked Trout with Lemon Sauce

Trout Fillets

2   pounds trout fillets
    Salt and pepper
4   green onions, chopped (white
      and green parts)

1   tablespoon finely chopped
      fresh parsley
    Paprika

Lemon Sauce

4   tablespoons (½ stick)
      margarine, melted

2   tablespoons lemon juice
2   cloves garlic, minced

Preheat oven to 375 degrees. Cover a baking sheet with aluminum foil; place fillets on foil; season with salt and pepper. Sprinkle green onions, parsley, and paprika on fillets. Whisk together the sauce ingredients and pour over the prepared fish. Bake for about 25 minutes or until fish flakes easily. Baste with lemon sauce during cooking. Spoon lemon sauce over fish and serve hot.

Yield: 6 servings

Note: To determine if fish is cooked, prod with a fork at the thickest point. A properly cooked fish is opaque, has milky white juices, and just begins to flake easily. Undercooked fish is translucent and will have clear, watery juices.

Broiled Orange Roughy

2	pounds orange roughy fillets	3	tablespoons mayonnaise
2	tablespoons lemon juice	3	tablespoons chopped green onions (white and green parts)
½	cup Parmesan cheese	¼	teaspoon salt
4	tablespoons (½ stick) margarine, melted	¼	teaspoon black pepper

Preheat oven to 500 degrees. Place fillets in a single layer in a greased 13 x 9 inch baking dish. Brush with lemon juice. Let stand 10 minutes. In a small bowl, combine cheese and all remaining ingredients; set aside. Broil fillets 3 to 4 inches from heat for about 5 minutes. Spread with cheese mixture and broil for another 2 to 3 minutes, watching closely. Cook until fish flakes easily. Serve hot.

Yield: 6 servings

Note: This popular fish comes to us from the waters in New Zealand. It is low in fat, has firm white flesh, and a mild flavor. It can be poached, baked, broiled, or fried. This broiled version is easy to prepare and delicious.

Quick and Easy Shrimp Casserole

2	tablespoons chopped onion	1	(10¾ ounce) can cream of mushroom soup, undiluted
2	tablespoons chopped bell pepper	1	teaspoon Worcestershire sauce
2	tablespoons margarine	1	teaspoon lemon juice
1	(10 ounce) package frozen shrimp	½	teaspoon dry mustard
			Pepper
2	cups cooked rice	1	cup (4 ounces) grated Cheddar cheese

Preheat oven to 350 degrees. In a medium skillet, sauté the onion and pepper in margarine, add shrimp and cook for 1 minute. Combine all the remaining ingredients and toss to mix. Place shrimp mixture into a greased 1½ quart casserole and bake uncovered for about 40 minutes. Serve hot.

Yield: 6 servings

Veracruz Fish

½ cup olive oil, divided
1 large onion, chopped
1 small bell pepper, chopped
2 cloves garlic, minced
3 stems fresh cilantro
3 stems fresh parsley
1 teaspoon salt
1 teaspoon black pepper
1 chicken bouillon cube

2 bay leaves
⅛ teaspoon dried oregano
1 tablespoon Worcestershire sauce
1 (28 ounce) can diced tomatoes
Hot pepper sauce (optional)
2½ pounds white, skinless fish fillets
½ cup green olives

In a large skillet, heat ¼ cup olive oil. Sauté onion and the next 4 ingredients. Add salt, pepper, and the next 6 ingredients. Bring to a boil; reduce heat and simmer for 10 minutes. In a large skillet, brown fish in remaining olive oil for about 1 minute on each side. Add sauce and olives; simmer for about 8 minutes. Remove bay leaves and serve.

Yield: 6 servings

Note: This classic Mexican dish is easy to fix. Even if you don't like fish, I believe you will enjoy serving this recipe to your family and friends.

Baked Tuna Casserole

2 (12 ounce) cans Albacore tuna
2 cups chopped celery
½ cup chopped sweet pickles
3 tablespoons grated onion
3 tablespoons lemon juice

1½ cups mayonnaise
1 cup (4 ounces) grated Cheddar cheese
1½ cups crushed potato chips

Preheat oven to 450 degrees. Drain and flake tuna. In a large bowl, combine the tuna and the next 5 ingredients; toss ingredients to mix. Spoon mixture into lightly greased individual bakers or a 3 quart greased casserole dish. Sprinkle with cheese and crushed potato chips. Bake casserole uncovered for 10 minutes or until heated through.

Yield: 8 servings

 **Main Dishes**

Spicy Sautéed Fish and Tomatoes

2	pounds orange roughy fillets	¼-½	teaspoon dried crushed red
	Salt and pepper		pepper
¼	cup olive oil	4	cups cherry tomatoes, halved
½	cup chopped fresh parsley	1	cup black olives, sliced
		6	cloves garlic, minced

Season fish with salt and pepper. Heat olive oil in heavy large skillet over medium-high heat; add half of fish to skillet and sauté until just opaque in center, about 3 minutes per side. Transfer fish to platter. Repeat with remaining fish. Add parsley and crushed red pepper to same skillet; sauté 1 minute. Add tomatoes, olives, and garlic; sauté until tomatoes are soft and juicy, about 2 minutes. Spoon sauce over fish and serve.

Yield: 4 servings

Salmon Loaf

1	(15 ounce) can salmon, drained	1	cup bread crumbs
½	cup milk	½	teaspoon salt
2	eggs, beaten	¼	teaspoon black pepper
1	cup (4 ounces) grated Cheddar cheese	2	tablespoons dried parsley
½	cup chopped ripe olives, drained (optional)	2	tablespoons dried, minced onions

Preheat oven to 350 degrees. In a large bowl, combine salmon, milk, and eggs; stir to blend. Add cheese and all remaining ingredients. Stir to blend thoroughly. Shape into a loaf and press mixture into a greased 9 x 5 inch loaf pan. Bake uncovered for 30 minutes. Let set for a few minutes; slice and serve.

Yield: 4 servings

Desserts

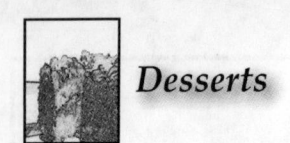

Desserts

Cakes

Pies and Cheesecakes

Cookies and Bars

Puddings and Desserts

 *Desserts*

Pound Cake

2	sticks butter, softened	½	teaspoon baking powder
½	cup solid vegetable shortening	1	cup milk
3	cups sugar	1	teaspoon vanilla extract
5	eggs	1	teaspoon almond extract
3	cups cake flour		

Cream together butter and shortening. Add sugar and continue to cream until perfectly smooth, about 10 minutes. Add eggs one at a time, beating until well blended. Sift together the flour and baking powder. Add dry ingredients a little at a time to creamed mixture. Slowly add milk, then extracts. Spoon batter into a greased and floured Bundt pan or a large tube pan that has bottom lined with wax or parchment paper and has been greased and floured. Place into a cold oven. Set temperature at 350 degrees and bake for 1 hour and 15 minutes or until top springs back when touched. Cool slightly and remove from pan.

Yield: 16 servings

Note: This cake has a fabulous texture. It has all of the basic ingredients of a modern pound cake, but is superior to most I have tested. When the cake is made with cake flour the texture is like velvet.

White Chocolate Pound Cake

Cake

8	(1 ounce) squares white baking chocolate, divided
2	sticks butter, softened
2	cups sugar
5	eggs
2	teaspoons vanilla extract
½	teaspoon almond extract

3	cups all-purpose flour
1	teaspoon baking powder
¼	teaspoon baking soda
½	teaspoon salt
1	cup sour cream
2	tablespoons sugar

Glaze

4	(1 ounce) squares semisweet baking chocolate, melted

4	(1 ounce) squares white baking chocolate, melted

Preheat oven to 350 degrees. Chop four squares of white chocolate and melt the other four; set both aside. In a large mixing bowl, cream butter and sugar until light and fluffy, about 5 minutes. Add eggs, one at a time, beating well after each addition. Stir in extracts and melted chocolate. Sift together the flour, baking powder, soda, and salt; add to the creamed mixture alternately with sour cream. Beat just until combined. Grease a 10 inch fluted tube pan. Sprinkle with the 2 tablespoons sugar. Pour a third of the batter into the pan. Sprinkle with half of the chopped chocolate. Repeat. Pour remaining batter on top. Bake for 1 hour or until cake tester inserted near the center comes out clean. Cool for 10 minutes; remove from pan and drizzle semisweet and white chocolate over cake.

Yield: 16 servings

Note: White chocolate is not considered true chocolate because it contains no chocolate and very little chocolate flavor. It is a mixture of sugar, cocoa butter, milk solids, lecithin, and vanilla. Unless the label mentions cocoa butter, it is not white chocolate but a confectionery coating and will not work in this recipe.

 *Desserts*

Coconut Pound Cake

6	eggs, separated	½	teaspoon coconut flavoring
1	cup solid vegetable shortening	3	cups sifted all-purpose flour
1	stick margarine, softened	1	cup milk
3	cups sugar	2	cups flaked coconut
½	teaspoon almond extract		

Preheat oven to 300 degrees. Separate eggs, placing whites into a large bowl, yolks into another large bowl. Let egg white warm to room temperature, about 1 hour. With electric mixer at high speed, beat egg yolks with shortening and margarine until well blended. Gradually add sugar; beat until light and fluffy. Add almond extract and coconut flavoring; beat until blended. At low speed, beat in flour alternately with milk, beginning and ending with flour. Add coconut; beat until well blended. Beat egg white just until stiff peaks form. With wire whisk or rubber scraper, gently fold whites into batter until well combined. Pour batter into a 10 inch greased and floured tube pan. Bake for 2 hours or until cake tester inserted near center comes out clean. Cool in pan on wire rack for 15 minutes. Remove cake from pan.

Yield: 16 servings

Note: Here is my favorite coconut pound cake recipe. I have made this cake for over 30 years now. Since the egg whites are added separately, the cake top will have a macaroon texture when baked.

Fresh Apple Cake Supreme

5-6	red delicious apples	2	teaspoons baking soda
3	cups sugar	½	teaspoon salt
2	eggs, beaten	½	teaspoon ground cinnamon
2	teaspoons vanilla extract	½	teaspoon ground nutmeg
1	cup vegetable oil	1½	cups chopped pecans
3	cups all-purpose flour		

Preheat oven to 325 degrees. Peel apples and chop fine. Add the sugar and soak for 2 to 3 hours. Stir in eggs, vanilla extract, and oil. Sift together the flour and the next 4 ingredients; add to the apple mixture and beat until well blended. Stir in pecans. Pour into a greased and floured Bundt pan or angel food cake pan. Bake 1 to 1½ hours or until cake tester inserted near center comes out clean. Cool in pan on wire rack 15 minutes; remove from pan and serve.

Yield: 12 servings

Note: This is an extremely moist cake. If using a Bundt pan, be sure the creases are well greased and floured to prevent sticking. If using an angel food cake pan, line bottom with wax paper and grease and flour pan.

Texas Sausage Cake

3 cups (packed) light brown sugar	¼ teaspoon salt
	2 teaspoons ground cinnamon
1 pound lean bulk pork sausage, mildly-flavored	1 teaspoon ground nutmeg
	1 cup strong black coffee
1 egg, beaten	2 teaspoons vanilla extract
3¼ cups all-purpose flour	½ cup raisins
3 teaspoons baking powder	1 cup chopped pecans
2 teaspoons baking soda	2 tablespoons all-purpose flour

Preheat oven to 350 degrees. Mix the brown sugar and sausage together; add egg and stir to blend. Sift together the flour and the next 5 ingredients; add to sausage mixture, alternately with coffee. Stir in vanilla extract and beat mixture well. Toss the raisins, pecans, and flour together; add to cake mixture. Stir to combine. Pour mixture into a well greased and floured tube pan with bottom lined with wax or parchment paper. Bake for 1 hour and 15 minutes or until cake tester inserted into center comes out clean. Allow to cool a few minutes before removing from pan.

Yield: 16 servings

Note: The Texas Agriculture Department printed this recipe a number of years ago. It is a wonderful cake to serve in the fall when the weather turns cooler. It is a heavy cake with a wonderful spicy flavor. No, you don't taste the sausage in the cake!

Old South Mincemeat Cake

1 (27 ounce) jar prepared mincemeat	2 cups sugar
1 (15 ounce) box seedless raisins	3 eggs, separated
2 cups chopped pecans	1½ teaspoons baking soda
1 tablespoon vanilla extract	¼ cup water
1 stick margarine, softened	3 cups all-purpose flour

Preheat oven to 275 degrees. In a large mixing bowl, combine mincemeat, raisins, pecans, and vanilla extract; set aside. In another large mixing bowl, cream margarine until light and fluffy, add sugar and continue beating until well blended; add egg yolks; beat well. Combine baking soda and water; add to mixture. Sift flour over mincemeat mixture; stir to mix well. Combine contents of both bowls; mix well. Batter will be stiff. In small bowl of mixer, beat egg whites until stiff, but not dry. Fold into batter. Spoon batter into a greased and floured 10 inch tube pan with bottom lined with wax or parchment paper. Bake for 2 to 2½ hours, or until done. Cake will pull away from sides of pan slightly when done. Cool slightly; remove from pan.

Yield: 16 servings

Note: To fold in egg whites, first lighten the batter by mixing in a quarter of the whites. Then add the remaining whites and gently cut them into the batter with a rubber spatula, turning the bowl as you mix.

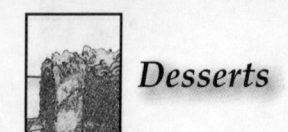

Orange Candy Slice Cake

Cake

2	sticks butter, softened	1	pound dates, finely chopped
2	cups sugar	1	pound orange slice candy, finely chopped
4	eggs	2	cups chopped pecans
1	teaspoon baking soda	1	cup flaked coconut
½	cup buttermilk		
4	cups unsifted all-purpose flour, divided		

Glaze

1	cup orange juice	1	cup unsifted powdered sugar

Preheat oven to 250 degrees. In a large mixing bowl, cream butter and sugar; add eggs one at a time, beating after each addition. Dissolve baking soda in buttermilk; add alternately to creamed mixture with 3½ cups flour. In a medium bowl, toss the remaining flour with the dates, orange slice candy, and pecans; add to batter with the coconut. Stir well to blend. Spoon batter into a 10 inch tube pan that has been greased and floured and the bottom lined with wax or parchment paper. Bake for 3 hours or until cake springs back when lightly pressed. While cake is baking, combine orange juice and powdered sugar; mix well. Immediately pour over hot cake in pan. Let stand in pan overnight before removing.

Yield: 16 to 20 servings

Note: This is a wonderful substitute for a Christmas fruit cake. To save time, cut the orange slices with kitchen scissors that have been dipped into flour.

Hummingbird Cake

Cake

3	cups all-purpose flour
2	cups sugar
1	teaspoon baking soda
1	teaspoon salt
1	teaspoon ground cinnamon
3	eggs, beaten
1	cup vegetable oil

1½ teaspoons vanilla extract
1 (8 ounce) can crushed pineapple, undrained
1 cup chopped pecans
2 cups (about 4 large) mashed ripe bananas

Cream Cheese Frosting

1 (8 ounce) package cream cheese, softened
1 stick margarine, softened

1 (1 pound) box powdered sugar, sifted
1 teaspoon vanilla extract
½ cup chopped pecans

Preheat oven to 350 degrees. In a large mixing bowl, sift together the flour and the next 4 ingredients. In a small bowl whisk together the eggs and vegetable oil; add to the dry ingredients and stir to moisten. Do not beat. Stir in vanilla extract, pineapple, pecans, and bananas. Spoon batter into 3 greased and floured 9 inch round cake pans. Bake for 25 to 30 minutes or until a cake tester inserted into the center comes out clean. Cool in pans 10 minutes; remove and cool completely. While cake is cooling, combine cream cheese and margarine, beat until smooth. Add powdered sugar and vanilla extract; beat until light and fluffy. Spread frosting between layers and on top and sides of cooled cake; sprinkle chopped pecans on top.

Yield: 12 servings

 *Desserts*

Christmas Coconut Cake

Cake

2	sticks margarine, softened	⅛	teaspoon salt
2	cups sugar	1	cup buttermilk
7	eggs	2	tablespoons vegetable oil
2¾	cups all-purpose flour	1	teaspoon vanilla extract
1	teaspoon baking powder	1	teaspoon coconut flavoring
1	teaspoon baking soda		

Coconut Frosting

1	cup milk	1	cup sugar
¼	cup all-purpose flour	1	teaspoon coconut flavoring
1	stick margarine, softened	1	teaspoon vanilla extract
½	cup solid vegetable shortening	2	cups flaked coconut, divided

Preheat oven to 350 degrees. In a large mixing bowl, cream margarine and gradually add sugar; beat 10 to 15 minutes at medium speed of electric mixer. Add eggs, one at a time, beating well after each addition. Sift together the flour, baking powder, baking soda, and salt; set aside. Whisk together the buttermilk and vegetable oil; add alternately to the creamed mixture with the dry ingredients, beginning and ending with flour mixture. Mix well after each addition. Stir in flavorings. Pour batter into 3 greased and floured 9 inch round cake pans. Bake for 20 to 25 minutes or until a cake tester inserted into the center comes out clean. Cool in pans 10 minutes; remove and cool completely. To prepare frosting, combine milk and flour in a medium saucepan; cook over medium heat, stirring constantly, until mixture thickens. Remove from heat and cool completely. Cream margarine, shortening, sugar, and flavorings together until fluffy. Add to flour and milk mixture. Beat until mixture is like whipped cream; fold in 1 cup coconut. Spread frosting between layers and on top and sides of cake; then sprinkle the remaining coconut on top and sides of cake.

Yield: 16 servings

White Chocolate Cake

Cake

3	sticks margarine	3½	cups all-purpose flour, divided
¾	cup water		
4	(1 ounce) squares white baking chocolate, chopped	1	cup toasted chopped pecans
		2¼	cups sugar
1½	cups buttermilk	1	teaspoon baking powder
4	eggs, slightly beaten	1	teaspoon baking soda
¼	teaspoon rum extract	½	cup flaked coconut

White Chocolate Frosting

4	(1 ounce) squares white baking chocolate, chopped	1	(8 ounce) package cream cheese
1	stick margarine, softened	1	(3 ounce) package cream cheese
		6	cups sifted powdered sugar

Preheat oven to 350 degrees. In a medium saucepan bring margarine and water to boiling, stirring constantly. Remove from heat and add chocolate. Stir until chocolate melts. Allow mixture to cool; stir in buttermilk, eggs, and rum extract; set aside. Toss ½ cup flour with the toasted pecans; set aside. Sift together the remaining flour, sugar, baking powder, and baking soda; stir in the coconut. In a large bowl, combine the dry ingredients with liquid ingredients; stir to combine. Fold in the pecans. Pour batter into 3 greased and floured 9 inch round cake pans. Bake 25 to 30 minutes or until a cake tester inserted into the center comes out clean. Cool in pans for 10 minutes. Remove from pans; cool completely on racks before frosting. To prepare the frosting, heat chocolate in the microwave oven until it melts; set aside to cool. In a large mixing bowl, combine the margarine and cream cheese; add chocolate and blend. Gradually add powdered sugar and beat until smooth. Spread frosting between layers and on top and sides of cake.

Yield: 16 servings

 *Desserts*

German Chocolate Cake

Chocolate Cake

1	(4 ounce) package German sweet chocolate
½	cup boiling water
2	sticks margarine
2	cups sugar
4	egg yolks

1	teaspoon vanilla extract
2	cups all-purpose flour
1	teaspoon baking soda
½	teaspoon salt
1	cup buttermilk
4	egg whites, stiffly beaten

Coconut Pecan Frosting

1	cup evaporated milk
1	cup sugar
3	egg yolks
1	stick margarine

1	teaspoon vanilla extract
1⅓	cups coconut
1	cup chopped pecans

Preheat oven to 350 degrees. Melt chocolate in water; cool. Cream margarine and sugar until fluffy. Add egg yolks, one at a time, beating well after each addition. Add chocolate and vanilla extract; mix well. Sift together flour, baking soda, and salt; add alternately with buttermilk to chocolate mixture; beating well. Fold in egg whites. Pour batter into three greased and floured 8 inch round cake pans, lined with wax or parchment paper. Bake 30 to 40 minutes or until a cake tester inserted into the center comes out clean. Cool layers on wire racks. To prepare frosting, combine milk, sugar, egg yolks, and margarine in a medium saucepan. Cook over low heat, stirring constantly until thickened, about 12 minutes. Add vanilla extract, coconut, and chopped pecans. Beat until thick enough to spread. Spread frosting between layers and on top and sides of cake.

Yield: 16 servings

Chocolatetown Special Cake

Cake

⅔ cup solid vegetable shortening	½ teaspoon salt
1¾ cups sugar	1½ cups buttermilk
2 eggs	1½ teaspoons baking soda
2½ cups all-purpose flour	1 teaspoon vanilla extract
½ cup cocoa	

Creamy Chocolate Frosting

9 ounces semisweet chocolate, chopped	1 (8 ounce) package cream cheese, softened
4 tablespoons (½ stick) margarine	1 teaspoon vanilla extract
	2¼ cups powdered sugar

Preheat oven to 350 degrees. In a large mixing bowl, cream the shortening with the sugar; add eggs one at a time and beat until fluffy; set aside. In another bowl, sift together the flour, cocoa, and salt; set aside. Combine the buttermilk and baking soda; add alternately to the creamed mixture with the flour mixture, beginning and ending with the flour mixture. Stir in the vanilla extract. Spoon batter into 2 greased and floured 9 inch round cake pans that have been lined with wax or parchment paper. Bake for 25 to 30 minutes or until a cake tester inserted into the center comes out clean. Remove from pans and cool on wire racks. While the cake is cooling, prepare the frosting. In a heavy medium saucepan over low heat melt the chocolate and margarine together. Set aside and cool to lukewarm. In a large bowl beat the cream cheese until fluffy. Gradually add lukewarm chocolate mixture, then vanilla extract, beating until smooth. Gradually add powdered sugar, beating until well blended. Spread frosting between layers; then frost top and sides of cake.

Yield: 16 servings

Note: Old-fashioned chocolate cake defines Americana at its best. My mother often made this cake for my sister and I when we needed a cake for special occasions. She cooked the icing rather than using the quick recipe above. The original recipe is from Hershey's Cocoa box and dates back at least half a century.

 *Desserts*

Spice Cake with Orange Frosting

Cake

2	cups all-purpose flour
1	teaspoon baking powder
1	teaspoon baking soda
½	teaspoon salt
1	teaspoon ground cinnamon
1	teaspoon ground nutmeg
1	teaspoon ground ginger

1	teaspoon ground cardamom
2	cups sugar
2	sticks margarine, softened
1	tablespoon grated orange rind
4	eggs
1	cup sour cream
½	cup milk

Orange Cream Cheese Frosting

1	(8 ounce) packages cream cheese, softened
1	stick margarine, softened
3	cups powdered sugar

2	teaspoons grated orange rind
1	teaspoon vanilla extract
⅓	cup sour cream

Preheat oven to 350 degrees. Sift together into a medium bowl the flour, and the next 7 ingredients; set aside. Using electric mixer, cream the sugar, margarine, and grated orange rind until fluffy. Beat in eggs 1 at a time. Stir flour mixture into creamed mixture alternately with sour cream and milk; beat until smooth and well blended. Spoon batter into three greased and floured 9 inch round cake pans lined with wax or parchment paper. Bake 25 minutes or until cake tester inserted into center comes out clean. Remove cake from pans and cool completely on racks before frosting. Using electric mixer, beat cream cheese and margarine in large bowl until well blended. Add sugar, orange rind, vanilla extract and sour cream; beat until smooth. Spread frosting between layers; then frost top and sides of cake.

Yield: 16 servings

Strawberry Cake

Cake

1   (3 ounce) box strawberry
     gelatin
½   cup boiling water
3   eggs, beaten
½   cup vegetable oil

½   (10 ounce) box frozen
     strawberries, thawed, crushed
1   (l pound, 2 ounce) box white
     cake mix

Frosting

½   (10 ounce) box frozen
     strawberries, thawed, crushed

1   stick margarine, softened
1   (l pound) box powdered sugar

Preheat oven to 350 degrees. Dissolve strawberry gelatin in water; set aside; cool. In a large mixing bowl, combine gelatin mixture and all remaining ingredients; beat with electric mixer for 5 minutes or until mixture is thoroughly blended. Spoon mixture into a greased and floured 13 x 9 inch baking pan or three (8 inch) round cake pans. Bake for 35 to 40 minutes for oblong pan or 25 to 30 minutes for round cake pans. Cool round pans for 10 minutes before turning cake out on racks to cool. Cool completely before frosting. To prepare frosting, combine all ingredients in a large mixing bowl; beat on high speed of mixer until well blended and fluffy. Spread frosting between layers; then frost top and sides of cake.

Yield: 16 servings

Note: Sift powdered sugar on plate before placing fresh cake on it, to prevent the cake from sticking to the plate.

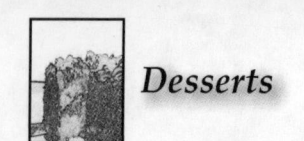 *Desserts*

Banana Cake
with Sour Cream Frosting

Banana Cake

2	cups all-purpose flour	2	eggs
½	teaspoon baking powder	¾	cup sour cream
¾	teaspoon baking soda	1⅓	cups (about 3 large) mashed ripe bananas
½	teaspoon salt	2	tablespoons fresh lemon juice
1	stick margarine, softened		
1½	cups sugar		

Sour Cream Frosting

½	cup sour cream	1	(8 ounce) package cream cheese, softened
2	cups powdered sugar		

Preheat oven to 350 degrees. In a medium bowl, sift together the flour, baking powder, baking soda, and salt; set aside. Using electric mixer, cream the margarine and sugar in a large bowl; add eggs and beat until fluffy. Mix in sour cream, bananas, and lemon juice. Add dry ingredients to banana mixture and beat until well blended. Spoon batter into a 13 x 9 inch baking pan that has been greased and floured. Bake cake for 30 minutes or until cake tester inserted into center comes out clean. Cool cake completely. Prepare frosting by beating sour cream, powdered sugar, and cream cheese together in a large bowl until well blended and fluffy. Spread frosting over cooled cake.

Yield: 12 servings

Hospitality Cake

Pineapple Cake

2	cups all-purpose flour
1½	cups sugar
1	teaspoon baking soda
½	teaspoon salt
2	eggs, beaten

2	cups crushed pineapple, slightly drained
½	cup (packed) light brown sugar
½	cup chopped pecans

Topping

1	stick margarine
¾	cup sugar

½	cup evaporated milk
½	teaspoon vanilla extract

Preheat oven to 325 degrees. In a large bowl, sift together the flour, sugar, baking soda, and salt; set aside. In a small bowl, combine the eggs and pineapple; stir into the dry ingredients; blend. Pour mixture into a greased and floured 13 x 9 inch pan. In a separate bowl, mix the brown sugar and pecans. Sprinkle over batter. Bake for 30 minutes or until top springs back when lightly touched. Begin making topping about 10 minutes before cake is done. In a small saucepan, combine the margarine, sugar, and evaporated milk. Bring mixture to a boil and cook over medium-low heat for about 3 minutes. Remove from heat; add vanilla extract. Spoon ½ of the topping over hot cake; allow cake to cool slightly and spoon remaining topping over cake.

Yield: 12 servings

Note: A (20 ounce) can of crushed pineapple slightly drained is equivalent to 2 cups of pineapple.

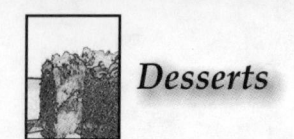 *Desserts*

Carrot Cake

Cake

2	cups all-purpose flour
2	teaspoons baking soda
2	teaspoons ground cinnamon
¼	teaspoon salt
3	eggs, beaten
¾	cup vegetable oil
¾	cup buttermilk
1½	cups sugar

2	teaspoons vanilla extract
1	(8 ounce) can crushed pineapple, undrained
2	cups grated carrots
1	cup flaked coconut
1	cup chopped pecans
1	cup raisins (optional)

Frosting

1	(3 ounce) package cream cheese, softened
4	tablespoons (½ stick) margarine, softened

3	cups powdered sugar, sifted
1-2	tablespoons milk
1	teaspoon vanilla extract

Preheat oven to 350 degrees. Sift together the flour, baking soda, cinnamon, and salt; set aside. In a large bowl, combine the eggs and the next 4 ingredients; mix well. Add the flour mixture and stir to blend. Add all remaining ingredients; stir to combine. Spoon mixture into a greased and floured 13 x 9 inch baking pan. Bake for 50 to 60 minutes or until top springs back when lightly touched. Cool completely; frost. To prepare the frosting, beat together cream cheese and margarine until fluffy. Alternately add the sugar, milk, and vanilla extract; continue beating until frosting is smooth. Frost cake.

Yield: 12 to 15 servings

Oatmeal Spice Cake

Cake

1½	cups boiling water	¼	teaspoon ground ginger
1	cup quick cooking oats	¼	teaspoon ground cloves
1½	cups sifted all-purpose flour	¼	teaspoon ground allspice
1	teaspoon baking soda	1	stick margarine
½	teaspoon salt	1	cup sugar
1½	teaspoons ground cinnamon	1	cup (packed) light brown sugar
½	teaspoon ground nutmeg	1	teaspoons vanilla extract
¼	teaspoon ground mace	2	eggs

Frosting

1	stick margarine	½	teaspoon vanilla extract
1	cup (packed) light brown sugar	1	cup chopped pecans
5	tablespoons evaporated milk	1½	cups coconut

Preheat oven to 350 degrees. In a small bowl, pour water over oats; cover and let stand for 20 minutes. Sift together into a large bowl the flour and the next 8 ingredients; set aside. Cream the margarine and sugars together; add the vanilla extract and eggs; beat until fluffy. Stir in the oat mixture. Add the flour mixture and beat until well blended. Pour batter into a well greased and floured 9 inch square baking pan. Bake for 50 to 55 minutes or until top springs back when lightly touched. Prepare frosting 10 minutes before cake is done. Combine the margarine, sugar, and milk in a small saucepan; cook for about 3 minute over low heat. Remove from heat; add vanilla extract, pecans, and coconut; stir to blend. Spread icing over hot cake.

Yield: 9 servings

Note: This is one of my favorite quick cake recipes. I have used my copy of this recipe so often it's falling apart. The original recipe came from a student I taught in the mid-1960s.

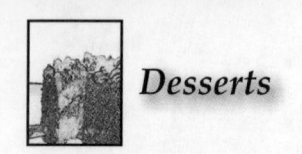 *Desserts*

Texas Pecan Pie

3	eggs	1	teaspoon vanilla extract
1	cup sugar	1½	cups chopped pecans
1	cup white corn syrup	1	(8 inch) unbaked pastry shell
4	tablespoons (½ stick) margarine, melted		

Preheat oven to 350 degrees. In a large mixing bowl, whisk the eggs; add sugar, corn syrup, margarine, and vanilla extract; stir to blend. Add pecans; stir and pour mixture into unbaked pastry shell. Bake for 45 to 60 minutes or until pie barely shakes in the middle.

Yield: 8 servings

Note: For the best quality pies, use aluminum pans with a dull finish or heat proof glass pie plates. Shiny metal pans do not bake the bottom crust well.

Oatmeal Pie

2	eggs, beaten	1	teaspoon vanilla extract
½	cup milk	¾	cup quick cooking oats
1	cup sugar	½	cup coconut
¾	cup dark corn syrup	1	(9 inch) unbaked pastry shell
4	tablespoons (½ stick) margarine, melted		

Preheat oven to 350 degrees. In a large bowl, combine the eggs and next 5 ingredients; blend well. Stir in the oats and coconut; blend. Pour filling into pastry shell. Bake for 50 to 60 minutes or until a knife inserted into the center comes out clean.

Yield: 8 servings

Note: This pie tastes similar to pecan pie. A dietitian friend shared this recipe with me years ago.

Fabulous Chocolate Pecan Pie

Spiced Crust

2	cups all-purpose flour	¼	teaspoon ground allspice
2	teaspoons sugar	¾	cup solid vegetable shortening
1	teaspoon ground cinnamon	6	tablespoons cold water

Chocolate Pecan Pie Filling

1½	cups pecan halves	3	eggs, beaten
1	cup semisweet chocolate pieces	1	cup dark corn syrup
2	tablespoons margarine, melted	1	tablespoon vanilla extract
1	cup sugar	1	teaspoon grated lemon rind
		⅛	teaspoon ground nutmeg

In a medium-size bowl, combine the flour, sugar, cinnamon, and allspice. Cut in shortening until mixture resembles coarse crumbs. Gradually sprinkle in cold water while kneading by hand. Roll dough into a ball; wrap in wax paper and chill at least 1 hour. Preheat oven to 375 degrees. Roll dough on a lightly floured board to fit a 9 inch pie plate. Ease pastry into pie plate; trim and flute edge. Place pecan halves and chocolate pieces over pastry. In a medium mixing bowl, combine margarine and the next 6 ingredients; stir to blend. Pour mixture into pie crust. Bake for 15 minutes. Reduce oven temperature to 350 degrees and bake 30 minutes or until a knife inserted near the center comes out clean. Cool pie before serving.

Yield: 8 servings

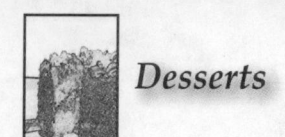

Old-Fashioned Chess Pie

2	cups sugar	1	stick margarine, melted
2	tablespoons all-purpose flour, heaping	3	eggs, beaten
1	tablespoon yellow cornmeal, heaping	½	cup buttermilk
		2	teaspoons vanilla extract
		1	(9 inch) unbaked pastry shell

Preheat oven to 425 degrees. In a large bowl, combine sugar, flour, and cornmeal; mix well. Add the margarine and stir to blend. Add eggs, buttermilk, and vanilla extract; thoroughly mix the ingredients. Pour mixture into pastry shell and bake for 10 minutes. Reduce temperature to 325 degrees and bake an additional 30 minutes. When pie begins to brown, cover with a sheet of aluminum foil to prevent deep browning. The pie is done when a knife inserted near the center comes out clean.

Yield: 8 servings

Note: This old Southern chess pie is probably my favorite pie. The simple filling can be varied by adding lemon flavoring in place of vanilla or by substituting brown sugar for granulated sugar.

Chocolate Chess Pie

1 cup sugar
3 tablespoons cornmeal
3 tablespoons cocoa
3 eggs, beaten

1 stick margarine, melted
½ cup light corn syrup
1 teaspoon vanilla extract
1 (8 inch) unbaked pastry shell

Preheat oven to 325 degrees. In a large mixing bowl, combine sugar, cornmeal, and cocoa; stir to blend. Combine eggs, margarine, corn syrup, and vanilla extract in a small bowl; add to the dry ingredients and mix well. Pour mixture into pastry shell and bake for 45 minutes or until knife inserted into center comes out clean.

Yield: 8 servings

Note: Both chocolate and cocoa powder come from beans that grow in pods on the cocoa tree. The beans are fermented, dried, roasted, and cooked. The inner part of the bean called nibs are ground and cocoa butter is extracted, leaving a paste called chocolate liquor. The liquor is dried and ground into cocoa powder.

Sweet Potato Cream Pie

1 (9 inch) pastry shell
1½ cups canned sweet potatoes, mashed
⅔ cup sugar
2 tablespoons margarine, melted
½ teaspoon ground nutmeg

½ teaspoon ground mace
½ teaspoon salt
½ teaspoon vanilla extract
2 tablespoons lemon juice
3 eggs, beaten
1 cup half-and-half
Whipped cream (optional)

Preheat oven to 450 degrees. Prick pastry shell on bottom and sides with a fork. Bake 10 minutes; remove from oven and reduce temperature to 375 degrees. Mix sweet potatoes and sugar. Add margarine and the next 5 ingredients; mix well. In a small bowl whisk together the eggs and half-and-half. Add egg mixture to potato mixture and mix until smooth. Pour mixture into partially baked pastry shell. Bake pie for 35 to 40 minutes or until a knife inserted into center comes out clean. Cool and serve plain or with whipped cream.

Yield: 8 servings

Chocolate Chip Walnut Pie

2	eggs	1	cup chopped walnuts
½	cup all-purpose flour	1	teaspoon vanilla extract
½	cup sugar	1	(9 inch) unbaked pastry shell
½	cup (packed) light brown sugar		Whipped cream or ice cream
1	cup margarine, melted, cooled		(optional)
1	(6 ounce) package semisweet chocolate chips		

Preheat oven to 325 degrees. In a large bowl, beat the eggs until foamy. In a small bowl, combine the flour and sugars; stir to blend. Add flour mixture to eggs and beat until well blended. Add margarine, chocolate chips, walnuts, and vanilla extract; stir to combine. Pour mixture into pastry shell. Bake for 1 hour or until done. Serve warm with whipped cream or ice cream.

Yield: 8 or more servings

Note: Rich and delicious is how I would describe this dessert. Since this pie freezes well, it can be made ahead of time, frozen and then warmed in the oven before serving.

Peanut Butter Cream Pie

¾	cup sugar	½	cup creamy peanut butter
2	tablespoons cornstarch	1	teaspoon vanilla extract
2	egg yolks, beaten	1	(8 inch) pastry shell, baked
2	cups milk		Meringue

Preheat oven to 350 degrees. In a medium saucepan, combine the sugar and cornstarch; stir to blend. Whisk the egg yolks and milk together and slowly add to the sugar. Stir in the peanut butter; cook over low heat until thickened, stirring constantly, about 10 minutes. Remove from heat and add vanilla extract. Pour into baked pastry shell and top with meringue. Bake for 10 minutes or until meringue is light golden browned.

Yield: 8 servings

Blueberry Custard Pie
with Streusel Topping

Custard Filling

3   cups fresh blueberries

1   (9 inch) unbaked pastry shell

1   cup sugar

¼   cup all-purpose flour

3   egg yolks

1   cup sour cream

Streusel Topping

½   cup all-purpose flour

¼   cup sugar

4   tablespoons (½ stick)
      margarine, softened

Preheat oven to 425 degrees. Wash and drain blueberries; place blueberries into pastry shell. Blend the sugar and flour together; set aside. Beat the egg yolks and combine with the sour cream; stir in flour mixture. Pour mixture over blueberries. Bake for 30 minutes. Combine the flour and sugar; add the margarine and rub together until crumbly. Sprinkle topping over custard and bake an additional 15 minutes or until browned and custard has set. Cool before serving.

Yield: 8 servings

Note: You will enjoy serving this fantastic recipe. It can be made with other fresh fruits such as peaches or blackberries, but blueberries are best. This is an original recipe from a neighbor.

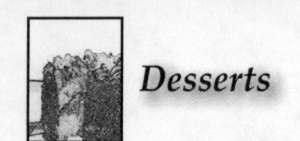 *Desserts*

Crunchy Dutch Apple Pie

Apple Pie

⅓	cup sugar	1	cup evaporated milk
¼	cup all-purpose flour	1	(21 ounce) can sliced pie apples
¼	teaspoon salt	1	(9 inch) unbaked pastry shell
1	teaspoon ground cinnamon		

Topping

½	cup (packed) light brown sugar	2	tablespoons margarine, softened
2	tablespoons all-purpose flour		
2	teaspoons ground cinnamon	½	cup chopped pecans

Preheat oven to 400 degrees. Mix together in a medium bowl the sugar, flour, salt, and cinnamon. Stir in the evaporated milk. Add apples with their syrup and stir gently to coat slices. Spoon mixture into pastry shell. Mix the sugar, flour, and cinnamon together; add the margarine and rub mixture together until crumbly. Add pecans and stir to blend. Sprinkle mixture over top of pie. Bake for about 45 minutes.

Yield: 8 servings

Fabulous Mincemeat Pie

Pastry For Two-Crust Pie

2 cups all-purpose flour	¼ cup cold water
1 teaspoon salt	1 tablespoon milk
⅔ cup, plus 2 tablespoons solid vegetable shortening	1 tablespoon sugar

Mincemeat Filling

1 (27 ounce) jar mincemeat pie filling	2 cups peeled and sliced cooking apples
1 (8 ounce) can crushed pineapple, drained	

Preheat oven to 425 degrees. In a medium bowl, combine the flour and salt; add shortening. With pastry blender, cut in the shortening. Sprinkle with the water and mix lightly with fork until all the flour is moistened. Gather dough together and press into a ball. Divide dough. Place larger half of dough on a lightly floured board and roll about 1 inch larger than pie plate. Gently lift pastry into pie plate; trim off overhanging edge. Mix together pie filling, crushed pineapple and apples. Spoon filling into crust. Roll out the remaining dough for the top crust, allowing edge to extend 1 inch beyond pan. Fold edge under and crimp with fingers. Brush top with milk and sprinkle with sugar. Make several slits near center to allow steam to escape. Bake 30 to 35 minutes. Shield edge of the pie with aluminum foil after 15 minutes to prevent excessive browning.

Yield: 8 servings

Note: I started using this pastry crust recipe as a teenager. It is tender and flaky. Avoid adding extra flour when rolling out the dough and handle gently for a superior crust. If preparing a double crust pie, brush the top with milk before baking. When baked the crust will be brown and glossy.

 *Desserts*

Old-Time Lemon Meringue Cream Pie

Never-Fail Meringue

1 tablespoon cornstarch	6 tablespoons sugar
2 tablespoons cold water	1 teaspoon vanilla extract
½ cup boiling water	⅛ teaspoon salt
3 egg whites	

Lemon Filling

1 cup sugar	3 tablespoons margarine
2 tablespoons cornstarch	1 teaspoon grated lemon rind
¼ teaspoon salt	⅓ cup lemon juice
2 cups milk	1 (8 inch) baked pastry shell
3 egg yolks, beaten	

Preheat oven to 350 degrees. In a small saucepan, blend cornstarch and water. Add boiling water and cook, stirring until clear and thick. Let stand until completely cold. With electric mixer at high speed, beat egg white in a medium bowl until foamy. Gradually add sugar and beat until stiff, but not dry. Turn mixer to low speed, add vanilla extract and salt. Gradually beat in cold cornstarch mixture. Turn mixer to high speed and beat well; set aside. To prepare filling, mix sugar, cornstarch, and salt in a medium saucepan. Add milk gradually and cook over low heat, stirring constantly, until thickened. Stir a small amount of hot mixture into egg yolks; combine with remaining hot mixture. Continue cooking, stirring constantly, about 5 minutes. Remove from heat; add margarine, lemon rind, and lemon juice; blend thoroughly. Pour into baked pastry shell and top with meringue. Bake for about 10 minutes or until meringue is light golden browned.

Yield: 8 servings

Note: This meringue takes a little more time to make than a traditional meringue; however, it is worth the extra effort. It cuts beautifully and never gets sticky.

Pineapple Cream Pie

1	cup sugar
¼	cup all-purpose flour
⅛	teaspoon salt
2	cups milk
3	egg yolks, beaten
2	tablespoons margarine

1	(8 ounce) can crushed pineapple, well drained
1	teaspoon vanilla extract
1	(9 inch) baked pastry shell
	Meringue

Preheat oven to 350 degrees. In a medium saucepan, combine the sugar, flour, and salt; add milk gradually and stir to blend. Cook over low heat, stirring constantly, until thickened, about 10 minutes. Stir a small amount of hot mixture into egg yolks, stir to blend. Combine egg yolks with remaining hot mixture; continue cooking, stirring constantly, about 5 minutes. Remove from heat; add margarine, pineapple, and vanilla extract. Pour into baked pastry shell and top with meringue. Bake for about 10 minutes or until meringue is light golden browned.

Yield: 8 servings

Note: The filling in this recipe can be used to make other cream pies. Omit the pineapple and add 3 large sliced bananas for banana cream pie or ¾ cup coconut for a coconut cream pie.

Sally's Chocolate Cream Pie

3	tablespoons cocoa	3	egg yolks, beaten
1	cup sugar	2	tablespoons margarine
6	tablespoons all-purpose flour	1	teaspoon vanilla extract
½	teaspoon salt	1	(9 inch) pastry shell, baked
2½	cups milk		Meringue

Preheat oven to 300 degrees. In a double boiler, combine cocoa, sugar, flour, and salt; stir to blend. Gradually whisk in milk. Cook until mixture thickens, stirring often. Combine a small amount of the hot mixture with the egg yolks; whisk to blend. Whisk egg mixture into pie filling; cook 2 minutes. Stir in margarine and vanilla extract; set aside to cool. Spoon pie filling into pastry shell; cover with meringue. Bake for 20 minutes or until light golden browned.

Yield: 8 servings

Note: Everyone loved my Mother's chocolate pie. She was still baking this pie at age 90 and taking it to special functions. It is included in this book by special request.

Cheesecake Supreme

Crust

1	cup all-purpose flour
¼	cup sugar
1	lemon (grated rind only)

1	stick margarine, softened
1	egg yolk

Cheesecake Filling

5	(8 ounce) packages cream cheese, softened
1¾	cups sugar
3	tablespoons all-purpose flour
1	lemon (grated rind only)

½	orange (grated rind only)
5	whole eggs
2	egg yolks
¼	cup heavy cream

Preheat oven to 500 degrees. Combine flour and sugar; add lemon rind and stir to blend. Add margarine and egg yolk. Mix with hands until well blended. Chill dough about 2 hours. Roll part of dough to ⅛ inch thickness; cut a round to fit bottom of a 10 inch springform pan; place on bottom of pan. Roll remaining dough into a strip and press onto sides of pan. Let ingredients, except heavy cream, stand at room temperature. In a large bowl, beat cheese until fluffy. Combine the sugar and flour; gradually blend into cheese. Add grated lemon and orange rinds. Add eggs and egg yolks one at a time, beating well after each. Stir in cream. Pour mixture into crust; set pan on a baking sheet and place into oven. Bake for 10 minutes; reduce heat to 200 degrees and bake approximately 1 hour and 20 minutes longer or until when shaken cheesecake remains firm. Remove from oven and place away from drafts until cooled. Refrigerate until cold.

Yield: 12 to 16 servings

Note: Cheesecakes occasionally crack on top. It helps to bake the cake in a moist oven and avoid opening the oven door. Do not over bake and cool slowly. To achieve a moist oven, place a 13 x 9 inch pan half filled with hot water on the bottom rack. Bake cheesecake on the middle rack. If the recipe calls for pre-baking crust, bake it before placing a pan of water into the oven.

Pumpkin Cheesecake

Graham Cracker Crust

1½	cups graham cracker crumbs	¾	teaspoon ground cinnamon
6	tablespoons (¾ stick) melted margarine	¼	teaspoon ground nutmeg

Pumpkin Filling

3	(8 ounce) packages cream cheese, softened	¼	teaspoon ground mace
		1	teaspoon salt
1½	cups sugar	2	teaspoons vanilla extract
3	tablespoons all-purpose flour	4	eggs
1½	teaspoons grated lemon rind	4	egg yolks
1½	teaspoons grated orange rind	1	(15 ounce) can pumpkin
½	teaspoon ground cinnamon		Sour cream
1	teaspoon ground cloves		Mandarin orange slices
1	teaspoon ground ginger		

Preheat oven to 350 degrees. Mix together thoroughly all the ingredients for the crust. Press on bottom of a 9 inch springform pan; set aside. Cream the cheese until light and fluffy. Combine the sugar and flour; gradually blend into the cheese. Add the lemon rind, and the next 7 ingredients and stir to blend. Add eggs and egg yolks one at a time, beating well after each. Stir in the pumpkin and beat until well blended. Pour mixture into crust; set pan on a baking sheet and place into oven. Bake for approximately 40 minutes or until, when shaken, cheesecake remains firm. Remove from oven and place away from draft until cooled. Refrigerate until cold; remove side of pan and place cake on serving plate. Garnish with sour cream and Mandarin orange slices.

Yield: 12 servings

Note: Be sure the ingredients for the filling are at room temperature before preparation begins. They will mix more easily and the finished cake will have a smoother texture. This is one of my all-time favorite recipes. It's a great recipe and life is too short not to eat cheesecake!

Lemon Cheesecake Squares

1 (1 pound, 2 ounce) box yellow cake mix, divided

4 eggs, divided

¼ cup vegetable oil

2 (8 ounce) packages cream cheese, softened

1 (14 ounce) can sweetened condensed milk

⅓ cup lemon juice

2 teaspoons grated lemon rind

1 teaspoon vanilla extract
Whipped cream
Lemon slices

Preheat oven to 300 degree. Remove ½ cup dry cake mix; set aside. Combine remaining cake mix, 1 egg, and oil in a large mixing bowl; mix well. Press mixture firmly on bottom and 1½ inches up sides of a greased 13 x 9 inch baking pan. In a medium bowl, beat the cream cheese until fluffy; gradually beat in sweetened condensed milk. Add remaining eggs one at a time and beat well. Add reserved cake mix and continue beating about 1 minute until well blended. Stir in lemon juice, lemon rind, and vanilla extract. Pour mixture into crust. Bake 50 to 55 minutes or until the center is just set. The cheesecake will have a dull, not shiny finish. Cool to room temperature, away from draft. Chill and cut into squares to serve. Garnish with whipped cream and lemon slices.

Yield: 12 to 15 servings

 *Desserts*

Brown Sugar-Oatmeal Cookies

1½ cups all-purpose flour	1 cup solid vegetable shortening
1 teaspoon baking soda	1 cup (packed) light brown sugar
½ teaspoon salt	1 cup sugar
1 teaspoon ground cinnamon	2 eggs
3 cups quick cooking oats	1 teaspoon vanilla extract

Preheat oven to 350 degrees. Sift together the flour, baking soda, salt, and cinnamon; stir in the oats; set mixture aside. Using electric mixer on medium-high speed, cream shortening and sugars in large bowl. Beat in eggs 1 at a time; add vanilla extract. Reduce speed to low; beat in dry ingredients. Drop dough by rounded tablespoonfuls onto lightly greased baking sheets, spacing mounds 1½ inches apart. Bake cookies until golden browned and crisp to touch, about 12 to 15 minutes. Let cool 5 minutes. Transfer cookies to racks; cool completely.

Yield: 3 dozen cookies

Note: This is an excellent cookie recipe. You can vary the recipe by adding 2 cups chopped pecans or 2 cups raisins.

Chocolate Chip-Oatmeal Cookies

1½ cups all-purpose flour
1 teaspoon baking soda
¾ teaspoon salt
2 cups old-fashioned oats
1 stick margarine, softened
½ cup solid vegetable shortening
1 cup (packed) golden brown sugar

1 cup sugar
2 eggs
1 teaspoon vanilla extract
1½ cups semisweet chocolate chips
½ cup chopped walnuts
½ cup raisins

Preheat oven to 350 degrees. In a small bowl, sift together the flour, baking soda, and salt; stir in oats; set mixture aside. Using electric mixer, cream margarine, shortening, and all sugar together. Add eggs one at a time to creamed mixture and beat well; add vanilla extract. Reduce speed to low; fold in dry ingredients. Add chocolate chips, walnuts, and raisins; stir to blend. Lightly grease baking sheets. Drop 1 rounded tablespoonful of dough onto sheet, spacing 1½ inches apart. Bake cookies until golden but still slightly soft to touch, about 15 minutes. Let cool 5 minutes; transfer cookies to racks; cool completely.

Yield: 3½ dozen cookies

White Chocolate Macadamia Cookies

2	cups all-purpose flour	½	cup sugar
1	teaspoon baking soda	1	egg
½	teaspoon salt	1½	teaspoons vanilla extract
1	stick margarine, softened	1	(6 ounce) package white chocolate chips
½	cup solid vegetable shortening		
¾	cup (packed) light brown sugar	1	(7 ounce) jar macadamia nuts

Preheat oven to 350 degrees. In a small bowl, sift together the flour, baking soda, and salt; set aside. Using electric mixer at medium-high speed, cream margarine, shortening, and sugars; beat in egg and vanilla extract. With mixer on low speed, add flour mixture and blend completely. Stir in chocolate chips and macadamia nuts. Drop by teaspoonfuls 2 inches apart on lightly greased cookie sheets. Bake cookies until golden but still slightly soft to touch, about 10 minutes. Cool cookies on baking sheets about 5 minutes; remove to racks and cool completely.

Yield: 5 dozen cookies

Note: Do not make the mistake of over baking cookies. They cook in a short time and a few degrees or minutes can make a difference. Watch for browning on the edges which indicates the cookies have finished baking.

Chocolate Chip-Walnut Cookies

5 cups all-purpose flour	1½ cups sugar
2 teaspoons baking soda	4 eggs
1 teaspoon salt	3 teaspoons vanilla extract
2 sticks margarine, softened	1 (12 ounce) package semisweet chocolate chips
1 cup solid vegetable shortening	2 cups coarsely chopped walnut pieces
1½ cups (packed) light brown sugar	

In a medium bowl, sift together the flour, baking soda, and salt; set aside. In a large mixing bowl, cream the margarine, shortening, and all sugar together on medium-high speed. Add eggs, one at a time to creamed mixture and beat well; add vanilla extract and blend. Turn mixer to low speed and blend in about half of the flour mixture; using a wooden spoon, stir in the remaining flour by hand. Add chocolate chips and walnut pieces; blend well. Chill dough for several hours or overnight. Preheat oven to 375 degrees. With a large scoop, place about ⅓ cup of dough for each cookie on an ungreased baking sheet. Bake for 10 to 12 minutes, until cookies are browned around the edges, but undercooked in center. Cool about 5 minutes on baking sheet and transfer to racks to cool completely.

Yield: 3½ dozen cookies

Note: These cookies are a chocolate lovers dream. Be sure to make them large by placing only a few scoops of dough at a time on a cookie sheet. Bake only one sheet at a time and refrigerate bowl of dough between pans.

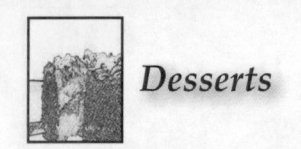 *Desserts*

Ranger Cookies

2	cups all-purpose flour	2	eggs
½	teaspoon baking powder	1	tablespoon vanilla extract
1	teaspoon baking soda	1	tablespoon butter flavoring
½	teaspoon salt	2	cups quick cooking oats
1	cup solid vegetable shortening	2	cups crisp rice cereal
1	cup sugar	1	cup coconut
1	cup (packed) light brown sugar	1	cup chopped pecans

Preheat oven to 350 degrees. In a small bowl, sift together the flour, baking powder, baking soda, and salt; set aside. In a large bowl with mixer at medium-high speed, cream the shortening and sugars together; add the eggs one at a time and beat well; add the vanilla extract and butter flavoring; beat until well blended. Turn mixer to low speed and blend in flour mixture. Using wooden spoon, stir in the oats, rice cereal, coconut, and pecans. Roll dough into 1 inch balls and bake on lightly greased baking sheets. Bake for 12 to 15 minutes or until golden browned. Cool on baking sheet for 5 minutes and then transfer to racks to cool completely.

Yield: 5 dozen cookies

Shirley's Sand Tarts

1	stick margarine, softened	2	cups all-purpose flour
¼	cup sugar	1	cup finely chopped pecans
1	teaspoon vanilla extract		Powdered sugar, sifted

Preheat oven to 300 degrees. In a large bowl, cream margarine and sugar together; add the vanilla extract and blend. Add flour and pecans; stir until well blended. Scoop a tablespoonful of dough, shape into a crescent; place dough on a lightly greased cookie sheet. Bake for 25 to 30 minutes or until lightly browned. Remove at once from the baking sheet and roll in sifted powdered sugar. Allow cookies to set a few minutes; roll a second time in powdered sugar and shake off excess sugar. Cool completely and store in airtight container.

Yield: 3 dozen cookies

All-Time Favorite Peanut Butter Cookies

2½ cups all-purpose flour
1 teaspoon baking soda
½ teaspoon salt
¾ cup solid vegetable shortening

1 cup creamy peanut butter
¾ cup (packed) light brown sugar
¾ cup sugar
2 eggs, beaten

Preheat oven to 350 degrees. In a small bowl, sift together the flour, baking soda, and salt; set aside. In a large bowl with mixer on medium-high speed, cream the shortening, peanut butter and sugars together. Add the eggs one at a time to the creamed mixture and blend well. Turn mixer to low speed and blend in the flour mixture. Roll the dough into 1 inch balls and place on ungreased cookie sheets. Flatten with a fork crisscross; bake for about 10 minutes. Remove from cookie sheets and cool completely on racks before storing in tightly covered container.

Yield: 2½ dozen cookies

Chocolate-Peanut Butter Bars

1⅔ cups graham cracker crumbs
1 (1 pound) package powdered sugar

2 sticks margarine, softened
1 cup creamy peanut butter
2 cups milk chocolate chips

In a large bowl, combine graham cracker crumbs, powdered sugar, margarine, and peanut butter; stir until well blended. Press dough on bottom of a 13 x 9 inch lightly greased baking pan; set aside. Melt chocolate chips in a double boiler or microwave oven. Spread chocolate over crust. Refrigerate until firm. Cut into 1½ x 3 inch squares.

Yield: 5 dozen bars

 *Desserts*

Breakfast Cookies

¾ cup whole wheat flour	1½ sticks margarine, softened
½ teaspoon baking soda	¼ cup (packed) light brown sugar
¼ teaspoon salt	⅓ cup honey
1 teaspoon ground cinnamon	2 eggs
1 teaspoon ground nutmeg	1 teaspoon vanilla extract
⅓ cup unprocessed bran	1 cup raisins
2 cups quick cooking oats	1 cup chopped pecans

Preheat oven to 350 degrees. In a small bowl, combine the flour, and the next 6 ingredients; stir to blend. In a large bowl, with mixer at medium-high speed, cream the margarine, sugar, and honey together; add the eggs one at a time and continue to beat until well blended; stir in the vanilla extract. Using a wooden spoon, stir in the flour mixture; add the raisins and pecans; stir until all ingredients are thoroughly blended. Drop by generous spoonfuls onto lightly greased baking sheets. Flatten to about ½ inch. Bake for 12 to 15 minutes or until lightly browned. Cool cookies on baking sheet about 5 minutes; remove to racks to completely cool. Store in airtight container.

Yield: 2 dozen cookies

Note: These cookies are not only a great treat, but are very nutritious. They are great for anyone who does not like to eat a traditional breakfast. Double the recipe and keep in freezer for later use.

Giant Gingersnaps

4½ cups all-purpose flour, divided	4 teaspoons ground ginger
2 teaspoons baking soda	1½ cups solid vegetable shortening
¼ teaspoon salt	2¾ cups sugar, divided
1½ teaspoons ground cinnamon	2 eggs
1 teaspoon ground cloves	½ cup molasses

Preheat oven to 350 degrees. In a medium bowl, sift together the flour and the next 5 ingredients; set aside. In a large bowl of an electric mixer, cream the shortening and 2 cups of sugar together; add eggs one at a time and beat well. Add the molasses and continue beating until mixture is completely blended. Turn mixer to low speed and add ½ of the flour mixture; beat until smooth. Stir in the remainder of flour with wooden spoon. Roll dough into 2 inch balls; roll in remaining sugar. Place cookies about 2 inches apart on ungreased cookie sheet; flatten slightly. Bake for 12 to 14 minutes; do not over bake. Remove from cookie sheet and allow to cool completely on wire rack. Store in airtight container.

Yield: 3½ dozen cookies

Note: Gingersnaps have been around American kitchens for a long time. This recipe with its old-fashioned taste is outstanding. It contains just the right proportion of ingredients to make a beautifully shaped cookie with a delicious flavor. These cookies may be frozen, if they don't disappear immediately after you bake them.

 *Desserts*

Holiday Sugar Cookies

Cookie Dough

3½ cups all-purpose flour	1½ cups sugar
1 teaspoon baking powder	2 eggs
½ teaspoon salt	1½ teaspoons vanilla extract
2 sticks margarine, softened	

Icing

1 tablespoon margarine, melted	½ teaspoon vanilla extract
1-2 tablespoons milk	1 cup powdered sugar, sifted

In a small bowl, sift together the flour, baking powder, and salt; set aside. In a large bowl, with the mixer at medium-high speed, cream together the margarine and sugar; add the eggs one at a time and beat well; stir in the vanilla extract. Turn mixer to low speed and blend in half of the flour. Stir in the remaining flour with a wooden spoon and blend thoroughly. Chill dough in refrigerator for several hours or overnight. Preheat oven to 400 degrees. Roll dough to ⅛ inch thickness on a lightly floured board, a little at a time; cut out with holiday cookie cutters. Bake for 8 to 10 minutes or until lightly browned. Remove from oven and cool completely on wire racks before frosting. To prepare the frosting, combine the margarine, milk, and vanilla extract; add powder sugar and blend until smooth. Spread on cooled cookies.

Yield: 3 dozen cookies

Note: This is one of those favorite recipes I have been using for many years. Don't think of this as just a Christmas cookie; cut in shapes for any special holiday. It is great plain or iced. Make ahead and freeze in an airtight container.

Spicy Walnut Triangles

2 sticks margarine, softened	2 cups all-purpose flour
1 cup sugar	1 teaspoon ground cinnamon
1 egg, separated	1 cup finely chopped walnuts

Preheat oven to 275 degree. In a large bowl, cream together the margarine and sugar. Add egg yolk; beat well. Sift together the flour and cinnamon; gradually add to creamed mixture, stirring well with a wooden spoon. Spread dough evenly into a 15 x 10 inch jelly roll pan. With a wire whisk, beat egg white slightly; brush over top of dough. Sprinkle with walnuts and press down gently. Bake for 1 hour. Remove from oven and cool for a few minutes. While still warm, cut into 24 (2½ inch) squares; cut diagonally across each square to make triangles. Remove from baking sheet and cool on wire racks. Store in airtight container.

Yield: 4 dozen cookies

Texas Pecan Bars

Crust

1 (1 pound 2 ounce) box yellow cake mix, divided	1 stick margarine, softened
	1 egg

Pecan Filling

⅔ cup reserved cake mix	3 eggs, beaten
½ cup (packed) golden brown sugar	1 teaspoon vanilla extract
	1 cup chopped pecans

Preheat oven to 350 degrees. Remove ⅔ cup of cake mix from box and set aside for filling. In a large mixing bowl, combine the remaining cake mix, margarine, and egg; mix until crumbly. Press dough into a lightly greased 13 x 9 inch pan. Bake for 15 minutes or until lightly browned. While crust is baking, prepare the filling. In a medium bowl, combine the reserved cake mix and brown sugar; stir to blend. Add eggs and vanilla extract; blend thoroughly. Stir in pecans. Pour filling over partially baked crust. Return to oven and bake 30 minutes or until filling is set. Cool and cut into bars.

Yield: 16 to 24 servings

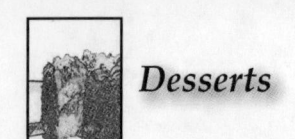 *Desserts*

Brown Sugar Shortbread Cookies

2	sticks butter, softened	¼	teaspoon salt
1	cup (packed) golden brown sugar	1	tablespoon sugar
2	cups all-purpose flour	1	teaspoon ground cinnamon

Preheat oven to 325 degrees. Using electric mixer, cream butter in a large bowl until light and fluffy. Add sugar and beat well. Using a wooden spoon, stir in flour and salt. Press dough into a lightly greased 9 inch springform pan. In a small bowl, combine the sugar and cinnamon; sprinkle over dough. Cut the dough into 12 wedges, cutting through dough. Pierce each wedge several times with toothpick. Bake shortbread for 1 hour or until lightly browned, firm at edges, and slightly soft in center. Cool completely in pan on wire rack. Remove pan sides; recut cookies into wedges. Store in airtight container at room temperature.

Yield: 12 servings

Note: Brown sugar is flavored with molasses. The difference between light brown, golden brown, and dark brown sugar is the amount of molasses each contains. A firmly packed cup of brown sugar may be substituted for 1 cup granulated sugar.

Raspberry Shortbread

Crust

1½	cups all-purpose flour	1	stick butter
½	cup sugar		

Filling

3	tablespoons all-purpose flour	1	teaspoon vanilla extract
¼	teaspoon baking soda	⅓	cup seedless raspberry jam
¼	teaspoon salt	1	cup chopped pecans
2	eggs		Powdered sugar (optional)
½	cup (packed) golden brown sugar		

Preheat oven to 350 degrees. In a medium bowl, blend the flour and sugar together. Add butter and cut into flour mixture with pastry blender until mixture resembles coarse crumbs. Line a 9 inch square baking pan with foil extending edges over sides. Press dough evenly onto bottom of pan. Bake for 20 to 25 minutes or until edges are golden. Cool pan on wire rack. In a small bowl, combine the flour, baking soda, and salt; blend well and set aside. In a medium bowl, beat the eggs, sugar, and vanilla extract together at medium-high speed. On low speed, beat in flour mixture just until blended. Spread the raspberry jam evenly over crust. Pour egg mixture on top; sprinkle with pecans. Bake for 25 minutes or until center is completely set and top is golden. Cool in pan on wire rack. Lift shortbread from pan. Peel off foil and cut into 16 squares, then half each square diagonally. Sprinkle with powdered sugar.

Yield: 32 shortbread triangles

Chocolate Chip-Macadamia Nut Bars

Shortbread Crust

1 cup all-purpose flour
¼ cup sugar

1 stick margarine, softened

Filling

1 cup sugar
½ cup all-purpose flour
2 eggs
4 tablespoons (½ stick) margarine, melted

1 teaspoon vanilla extract
1 cup miniature semisweet chocolate chips
1 cup coarsely chopped macadamia nuts

Preheat oven to 350 degrees. Mix flour and sugar together; add margarine; blend until mixture resembles coarse meal. Press mixture onto bottom and ¾ inch up sides of an 8 inch square glass baking dish. Bake for 15 minutes or until crust is golden browned on edges. In a medium bowl, combine sugar and flour; add the eggs, margarine, and vanilla extract. Stir until well blended. Stir in chocolate chips and macadamia nuts. Pour filling into warm crust. Bake 50 minutes or until filling is golden browned and tester inserted into center comes out with moist crumbs attached. Transfer dish to rack; cool completely. Cut into squares.

Yield: 16 squares

Chocolate-Coconut and Pecan Bars

1 stick margarine
1½ cups graham cracker crumbs
1 (14 ounce) can sweetened condensed milk

1 (6 ounce) package semisweet chocolate chips
1 (3½ ounce) can flaked coconut
1 cup chopped pecans

Preheat oven to 350 degrees. Melt the margarine in a 13 x 9 inch baking pan. Sprinkle graham cracker crumbs over melted margarine. Pour condensed milk evenly over crumbs. Top with chocolate chips, coconut, and pecans; press down gently. Bake for about 25 minutes or until golden browned. Cool in pan on wire rack. Cut into 1½ x 3 inch bars.

Yield: 24 bars

Fudge Oatmeal Squares

1	stick, plus 2 tablespoons margarine, divided
1	cup (packed) light brown sugar
1	egg
1	teaspoon vanilla extract
¾	cup all-purpose flour
½	teaspoon baking soda
½	teaspoon salt
2	cups quick cooking oats
1	(6 ounce) package semisweet chocolate chips
1	cup evaporated milk, undiluted
½	cup chopped walnuts
	Ice cream (optional)

Preheat oven to 350 degrees. Cream 1 stick margarine and the sugar together in a large bowl; add the egg and vanilla extract and beat until well blended. Sift together the flour, baking soda, and salt; add to the creamed mixture. Stir in the oats and mix well. Remove 1 cup of mixture and set aside. Spread the remaining mixture into a lightly greased 13 x 9 inch baking pan. Melt chocolate chips and remaining margarine in the microwave oven; stir in evaporated milk and walnuts. Pour over mixture in pan. Sprinkle with reserved oatmeal mixture. Bake for about 25 minutes. Cool pan for 15 minutes on wire rack. Cut into squares and serve with a scoop of vanilla ice cream or cool completely and serve as a moist cookie bar.

Yield: 12 servings

Chocolate-Pecan Brownies

1½	sticks margarine	3	eggs
4	ounces unsweetened chocolate, chopped	1	cup all-purpose flour
2	teaspoons instant espresso powder	½	teaspoon salt
		1	teaspoon vanilla extract
1	cup (packed) golden brown sugar	1	cup chopped pecans
		¾	cup semisweet chocolate chips

Preheat oven to 350 degrees. Stir margarine, chocolate, and espresso powder in heavy medium saucepan over low heat until mixture melts; set aside and cool. In a large bowl, combine the brown sugar and eggs; beat until very thick. Stir in the cooled chocolate mixture. Add the flour, salt, and vanilla extract; beat well. Stir in pecans and chocolate chips. Pour batter into a greased 9 inch square baking dish. Bake for 40 to 45 minutes or until tester inserted into center comes out with very moist crumbs attached. Cool completely; cut brownies into 3 inch squares.

Yield: 9 brownies

Brown Sugar Pecan Bars

1	stick margarine	1	teaspoon vanilla extract
1½	cups (packed) light brown sugar	1½	cups all-purpose flour
2	eggs	2	teaspoons baking powder
		1	cup chopped pecans

Preheat oven to 350 degrees. In a medium saucepan, melt the margarine; stir in sugar; add eggs one at a time beating well after each addition. Stir in the vanilla extract; set mixture aside. In a small bowl, sift together the flour and baking powder; stir into the creamed mixture. Add pecans and stir to blend. Spoon mixture into a lightly greased 13 x 9 inch baking pan. Bake about 30 minutes. Cool in pan on wire rack. Cut into 1½ x 3 inch bars. Store in airtight container.

Yield: 24 bars

Lemon Bars

Crust

1   (1 pound, 2 ounce) box lemon
   cake mix with pudding

1   egg, lightly beaten

1   stick margarine, melted

1   cup chopped pecans

Cream Cheese Filling

1   (8 ounce) package cream
   cheese, softened

2   eggs

1   (1 pound) box powdered sugar

Preheat oven to 350 degrees. In a large mixing bowl, combine the cake mix, egg, margarine, and pecans; mix ingredients together by hand. Dough will be stiff. Pat dough into a 13 x 9 inch lightly greased pan; set aside. In a large mixing bowl, with mixer on medium-high, beat the cream cheese with the eggs until well blended. Turn mixer to low and beat in the powdered sugar. Pour cheese mixture over the crust. Bake for 45 minutes or until golden browned.

Yield: 12 servings

 *Desserts*

Frosted Zucchini-Pecan Bars

Zucchini Bars

2   eggs
1   cup sugar
¾   cup vegetable oil
1½   teaspoons vanilla extract
1½   cups grated zucchini, loosely
    packed, drained
1½   cups all-purpose flour

1   teaspoon baking powder
½   teaspoon salt
1   teaspoon ground cinnamon
½   teaspoon ground allspice
½   teaspoon ground nutmeg
1   cup coarsely chopped pecans

Frosting

1   (3 ounce) package cream
    cheese, softened
2   cups powdered sugar, sifted

2   tablespoons milk
1   teaspoon vanilla extract

Preheat oven to 350 degrees. In a large mixing bowl, combine the eggs, sugar, vegetable oil and vanilla extract; beat together with electric mixer until blended. Stir in the zucchini. Set aside. Sift together the flour, and the next 5 ingredients. On low speed of mixer, combine the flour and the zucchini mixtures together until just blended. Add pecans. Pour batter into a greased and floured 13 x 9 inch baking pan; bake 30 to 35 minutes or until bars test done and are lightly browned on top. Cool bars in pan on wire rack. To prepare frosting, combine all the ingredients together in a medium bowl; blend until smooth. Spread over top of cooled bars. Cut into 2½ x 3 inch bars.

Yield: 15 bars

Kirby Hall's
Special Vanilla Dessert

Graham Cracker Crust

1½ cups graham cracker crumbs
¼ cup sugar
2 tablespoons all-purpose flour

6 tablespoons (¾ stick) margarine, melted

Vanilla Custard

2 cups hot milk
⅓ cup sugar
4 tablespoons cornstarch
¼ teaspoon salt
3 egg yolks, beaten

1 tablespoon margarine
1 teaspoon vanilla extract
Whipped cream (optional)
Maraschino cherries (optional)

Preheat oven to 350 degrees. In a medium bowl, combine the cracker crumbs, sugar, flour, and margarine; stir to blend. Pat the mixture onto the bottom and a little up the sides of a 8 inch pie plate. Bake 5 minutes. Remove from oven and cool while preparing vanilla custard. Heat the milk in a double boiler. While milk is heating, mix the sugar, cornstarch, and salt together in a small bowl. Remove a small amount of the hot milk and stir into the cornstarch mixture; whisk in the egg yolks. Add cornstarch and egg mixture to the hot milk slowly, stirring constantly. Cook until mixture thickens. Remove from heat and stir in margarine and vanilla extract. Cool custard for a few minutes and pour into crumb crust. Cool completely; cut into 6 slices. Garnish each slice with whipped cream and a Maraschino cherry.

Yield: 6 servings

Note: For many years, Kirby Hall was a Christian dormitory adjacent to The University of Texas campus in Austin. I lived there as a student until graduation in 1960. We always had wonderful meals and this seemed to be everyone's favorite dessert.

 *Desserts*

Vanilla Custard Flans
with Caramel Sauce

Custard Flans

4	cups half-and-half	⅔	cup sugar
8	large egg yolks	1	tablespoon vanilla extract

Caramel Sauce

¾	cup half-and-half	2	cups (packed) dark brown
1	tablespoon butter		sugar

Preheat oven to 325 degrees. Heat half-and-half in a 2 quart saucepan over medium heat until it begins to bubble at edges. Do not boil. Whisk egg yolks, sugar, and vanilla extract together in a large bowl. Gradually whisk in half-and-half. Divide mixture equally between 8 custard cups. Place cups into a large roasting pan. Add enough hot water to roasting pan to come halfway up sides of cups. Bake until flans are softly set, about 45 minutes. Carefully remove custard cups from roasting pan and cool. Cover and refrigerate overnight. To prepare caramel sauce, mix together the half-and-half, butter, and brown sugar in a heavy medium saucepan. Cook over medium heat until sugar dissolves, about 3 minutes. Do not boil. Cool sauce slightly and spoon warm sauce over flans and serve.

Yield: 8 servings

Cinnamon-Raisin
Bread Pudding with Rum Sauce

Bread Pudding

4 eggs
1¾ cups whole milk
1 cup sugar
¾ cup heavy cream

½ teaspoon vanilla extract
½ (1 pound) loaf cinnamon-swirl bread, cubed
½ cup golden raisins

Rum Sauce

1 cup (packed) golden brown sugar
2 tablespoons cornstarch
¼ teaspoon salt

2 cups boiling water
2 tablespoons margarine
2 teaspoons rum extract
½ teaspoon vanilla extract

In a large bowl, whisk the eggs; add milk, sugar, cream, and vanilla extract; whisk until well blended. Stir in bread cubes and raisins. Pour mixture into a buttered 13 x 9 inch glass baking dish; cover and refrigerate 2 hours. Preheat oven to 350 degrees. Bake pudding uncovered until puffed and golden, about 1 hour and 15 minutes. Pudding will fall as it cools. To prepare sauce, mix sugar, cornstarch, and salt together in heavy medium saucepan; gradually add water and stir to blend. Cook mixture until clear, stirring constantly. Remove from heat; add margarine, rum, and vanilla extracts; stir to blend. Serve warm with bread pudding.

Yield: 6 servings

Note: This simple, delicious dessert has long been a southern favorite. It can be served plain, with whipped cream, or a good sauce such as the one above.

Rice Pudding
with Vanilla Sauce

Rice Pudding

4	eggs, beaten	2	teaspoons vanilla extract
¾	cup sugar	2½	cups cooked rice
½	teaspoon salt	1	cup raisins
4	cups milk, scalded		Nutmeg

Vanilla Sauce

1	cup sugar	½	cup heavy cream
1	stick margarine	1	teaspoon vanilla extract

Preheat oven to 325 degrees. In a large bowl, combine eggs, sugar, and salt. Gradually add milk; add vanilla extract; stir to blend. Add rice and raisins. Pour mixture into a greased 2 quart baking dish. Sprinkle top with nutmeg. Set dish into a pan filled with 1 inch of hot water. Bake pudding 1½ hours, stirring after 30 minutes to prevent raisins from sinking to bottom. In a medium saucepan combine sugar and margarine; heat until margarine melts and mixture is smooth, about 2 minutes. Add cream and vanilla extract. Simmer until sauce thickens, about 5 minutes. Serve with warm rice pudding.

Yield: 8 servings

Fresh Lemon Custard Cups

1 cup sugar	5 tablespoons fresh lemon juice
¼ cup all-purpose flour	Grated rind of 1 lemon
⅛ teaspoon salt	3 eggs
2 tablespoons margarine, melted	1½ cups milk

Preheat oven to 350 degrees. In a medium bowl, combine the sugar, flour, and salt. Stir in the margarine, lemon juice, and lemon rind. Stir to blend. Separate the egg yolks from the whites; set whites aside. Beat the yolks; add milk and blend thoroughly. Gradually stir the liquid mixture into the sugar mixture; blend thoroughly. In a small bowl, beat the egg whites until stiff, but not dry; fold into custard mixture. Divide mixture between 8 greased custard cups. Place cups into a large baking pan; add enough hot water to pan to come half-way up sides of custard cups. Bake for about 45 minutes. When baked, each dessert will have custard on the bottom with sponge cake on top.

Yield: 8 servings

Note: To extract the most juice from lemons, warm lemons in the microwave oven for 10 to 15 seconds on high heat. Roll lemons back and forth on counter top while pressing firmly with the palm of your hand. Cut in half and squeeze out juice.

 *Desserts*

Elegant Christmas Pudding

Pudding

1½ cups crushed vanilla wafers	¼ teaspoon salt
1 tablespoon unflavored gelatin	4 eggs
¼ cup cold water	¼ teaspoon cream of tartar
2 cups milk	¾ teaspoon vanilla extract
1 cup sugar, divided	¼ teaspoon almond extract
1½ tablespoons cornstarch	

Whipped Cream Topping

1 cup heavy cream	Grated coconut
¼ cup sugar	

Spread the vanilla wafers on the bottom of a 10 inch springform pan; set aside. Sprinkle unflavored gelatin over top of water; set aside to dissolve. Heat the milk in a double boiler. While the milk is heating, combine ½ cup sugar, cornstarch, and salt in a small bowl. Remove a small amount of the hot milk and stir into the cornstarch mixture; blend thoroughly. Separate the eggs; set aside the whites. Beat yolks and whisk into the cornstarch mixture; stir slowly into hot milk. Cook until mixture thickens to consistency of boiled custard. Add gelatin; stir to blend. In a medium bowl beat the egg whites until frothy; add remaining sugar and cream of tartar; beat until stiff peaks form. Do not over beat. Stir in the vanilla and almond extracts. Gradually fold egg whites into hot custard. Spoon over vanilla wafer crumbs. Cool and refrigerate until set. In a medium bowl, whip cream until stiff; add sugar and stir to blend. Spread whipped cream over pudding. Sprinkle with grated coconut. Cut into wedges and serve.

Yield: 12 servings

Fresh Lemon and Berry Trifle

1 (16 ounce) angel food cake
1 (14 ounce) can sweetened condensed milk
2 teaspoons grated lemon rind
⅓ cup fresh lemon juice
1 (8 ounce) carton lemon yogurt

1 (8 ounce) container frozen whipped topping, thawed, divided
1 cup sliced fresh strawberries
1 cup fresh blueberries
1 cup fresh raspberries
½ cup flaked coconut, lightly toasted

Cut cake into bite-size pieces; set aside. In a medium bowl, combine condensed milk, lemon rind, lemon juice, yogurt, and 2 cups whipped topping; set aside. Place ⅓ of the cake pieces into a 4 quart trifle bowl; top with ⅓ of the lemon mixture. Sprinkle with strawberries. Repeat layers twice, using remaining cake pieces, lemon mixture, blueberries, and ending with raspberries. Spread remaining whipped topping over the raspberries; sprinkle with toasted coconut. Cover and chill several hours.

Yield: 16 to 18 servings

Note: Coconut can be toasted in a preheated 325 degree oven. Place coconut in a thin layer on a baking sheet. Toast 7 to 10 minutes. Check after 5 minutes to prevent burning.

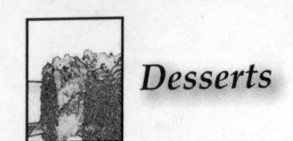 *Desserts*

Strawberry Kiss

3 egg whites
¼ teaspoon cream of tartar
⅛ teaspoon salt
¾ cup sugar

1 teaspoon vanilla extract
Vanilla ice cream
Fresh strawberries, sliced

Preheat oven to 400 degrees. Beat egg whites, cream of tartar, and salt until foamy. Gradually add sugar, about a tablespoonful at a time and beat until stiff peaks form. Fold in the vanilla extract. Spoon mixture into 8 mounds on a baking sheet lined with parchment paper. Spread each mound from the center with a spoon into a nest shape. Turn off oven. Place baking sheet into oven and leave for at least 8 hours or overnight. To serve, fill each shell with a scoop of vanilla ice cream and top with sliced strawberries.

Yield: 8 servings

Note: To produce a smooth meringue the sugar must be added gradually, about 1 tablespoonful at a time. Unlike the soft meringue used on pies, these shells are hard and must be baked longer and allowed to completely dry before filling.

Quick Berry Cobbler

1	stick margarine	2	teaspoons baking powder
1	cup all-purpose flour	⅔	cup milk
1½	cups sugar, divided	3	cups berries
½	teaspoon salt		Vanilla ice cream (optional)

Preheat oven to 350 degrees. Melt margarine in a 9 inch square baking dish. In a medium bowl, sift together the flour, 1 cup sugar, salt, and baking powder. Add milk and stir to combine ingredients. Pour batter over melted margarine. Mix berries and remaining sugar together in a large bowl. Sprinkle berries over top of batter. Bake for about 30 minutes or until firm and lightly browned. Serve plain or with a scoop of ice cream.

Yield: 6 to 8 servings

Note: This recipe can also be prepared with canned or frozen fruits. If canned fruit is used, drain fruit well and omit the ½ cup sugar used to coat berries. Frozen fruits should be thawed and drained. If fruit is frozen without sugar, toss with the ½ cup sugar.

Baked Bananas

6	bananas	2	tablespoon margarine, melted
⅓	cup (packed) light brown sugar	2	teaspoons rum extract
1	teaspoon grated orange rind		Vanilla ice cream
1½	teaspoons ground cinnamon		Cinnamon
¼	teaspoon ground nutmeg		

Preheat oven to 325 degrees. Peel and slice bananas lengthwise and cut into thirds. Place into a 11 x 7 inch glass baking dish that has been greased. Combine the sugar, orange rind, cinnamon, nutmeg, and margarine; stir to combine. Spread mixture over bananas. Bake for about 30 minutes; set aside to cool. To serve, divide bananas between 8 serving dishes and top with a scoop of vanilla ice cream. Garnish with additional cinnamon.

Yield: 8 servings

Note: Bananas can also be cooked in the microwave oven. Cover and cook on high power 2½ to 3 minutes. Avoid overcooking.

Pineapple and Blueberry Crunch

1	(20 ounce) can crushed pineapple, undrained	1	(1 pound, 2 ounce) box yellow cake mix
3	cups fresh or frozen blueberries	1	stick margarine, softened
1	cup sugar, divided	1	cup chopped pecans (optional)

Preheat oven to 350 degrees. Pour the crushed pineapple, including the juice over the bottom of a lightly greased 13 x 9 inch baking pan. Place the blueberries over the pineapple and sprinkle with ¾ cup sugar. In a large bowl, combine the cake mix and margarine; using a pastry blender, mix until it resembles coarse meal. Sprinkle the cake mixture over the fruit. Top with the chopped pecans and sprinkle with the remaining sugar. Bake for 35 to 40 minutes or until the top is bubbly and the cake tests done. Partially cool in pan on wire rack before serving. Cut into squares to serve.

Yield: 12 to 15 servings

Old-Fashioned Apple Crumble

5-6 Granny Smith apples, peeled, cored, sliced	¾ cup all-purpose flour
1 teaspoon ground cinnamon	1 cup sugar
½ teaspoon salt	5½ tablespoons margarine
¼ cup water	Vanilla ice cream (optional)

Preheat oven to 350 degrees. Prepare apples and place into a 11 x 7 inch greased baking dish. Sprinkle with cinnamon, salt, and water. Combine flour, sugar, and margarine; rub together with fingertips until crumbly. Sprinkle over apples. Bake until apples are tender, about 40 minutes. Allow to cool slightly. Divide equally between serving dishes and top with a scoop of vanilla ice cream.

Yield: 6 to 8 servings

Note: Apple varieties now number into the thousands. Some are better suited for baking than others. I like the Granny Smith, however other apples such as Gala are also well suited for baking. For baking whole the Rome Beauty is the apple of choice. It has deep red skin with yellow speckling and a firm mildly sweet flesh.

Pumpkin Crunch

3 eggs, beaten	1 (1 pound, 2 ounce) box yellow cake mix
1 (15 ounce) can pumpkin	
1 (12 ounce) can evaporated milk	1 stick melted margarine
1 cup sugar	1 cup chopped pecans
1½ teaspoons ground cinnamon	

Preheat oven to 350 degrees. In a large mixing bowl, combine the eggs and the next 4 ingredients; beat until mixture is smooth. Pour mixture into a greased and floured 13 x 9 inch baking pan. Sprinkle the dry cake mix on top of pumpkin mixture. Drizzle margarine on top of dry cake mix and sprinkle with chopped pecans. Bake for approximately 1 hour. Cool; cut into squares and serve.

Yield: 12 to 15 servings

 *Desserts*

Apple Dumplings

Dumplings

2	cups all-purpose flour	3	cooking apples, peeled, cored, sliced
2	teaspoons baking powder		
1	teaspoon salt	½	teaspoon sugar
⅔	cup solid vegetable shortening	¼	teaspoon ground cinnamon
½	cup milk		

Sauce

1½	cups sugar	1½	cups water
¼	teaspoon ground cinnamon	2	tablespoons margarine
¼	teaspoon ground nutmeg		

Preheat oven to 375 degrees. Sift together into a medium bowl the flour, baking powder, and salt; cut in shortening with pastry blender until mixture resembles coarse meal. Gradually add milk, stirring to make soft dough. Roll dough into an 18 x 12 inch rectangle on a lightly floured surface. Cut dough into six squares. Place 3 to 4 pieces of apple on each square. Moisten edges of each dumpling with water; bring corners to center, pinching edges to seal. Place dumplings into a lightly greased 11 x 7 inch baking dish. Combine the sugar and cinnamon; sprinkle evenly over top of dumplings. To prepare the sauce, combine the sugar and all remaining ingredients in a medium saucepan; cook over low heat, until the margarine melts and sugar dissolves. Pour syrup over dumplings. Bake for 45 minutes, basting once with syrup.

Yield: 6 servings

Gingerbread with Lemon Sauce

Gingerbread

1	stick margarine, softened	½	teaspoon salt
½	cup sugar	1	teaspoon ground cinnamon
1	egg	1	teaspoon ground cloves
1	cup molasses	1	teaspoon ground ginger
2½	cups sifted all-purpose flour	1	cup hot water
1½	teaspoons baking soda		

Lemon Sauce

½	cup sugar	2	tablespoons fresh lemon juice
1	tablespoon cornstarch	2	tablespoons margarine
1	cup boiling water	⅛	teaspoon ground nutmeg

Preheat oven to 350 degrees. In a large mixing bowl, cream the margarine and sugar together; add egg and molasses; continue beating until well blended. In a medium bowl, sift together the flour and the next 5 ingredients; add dry ingredients to creamed mixture. Add water and beat until smooth. Pour mixture into a greased and floured 9 inch square baking pan. Bake for 35 to 40 minutes or until a cake tester inserted into the center comes out clean. To prepare sauce, combine the sugar and cornstarch in a small, heavy saucepan. Add water slowly and stir to blend; boil for about 5 minutes until mixture thickens. Remove from heat; add lemon juice, margarine, and nutmeg; stir to blend. Serve warm sauce over gingerbread squares.

Yield: 9 servings

Chocolate Trifle

1	(19.8 ounce) box fudge brownie mix		8	(1.4 ounce) bars chocolate-covered toffee candy bars
3	(3 ounce) packages instant chocolate mousse		1	(12 ounce) container frozen nondairy whipped topping, thawed

Preheat oven to 350 degrees. Prepare and bake brownie mix according to package directions; set aside and cool. Prepare chocolate mousse according to package directions; set aside. Break the candy bars into small pieces in food processor or by gently tapping the wrapped bars with a hammer. Break up half the brownies into small pieces and place into a 4 quart trifle bowl. Cover with half the mousse, then half the candy and half the whipped topping. Repeat layers with the remaining ingredients. Refrigerate for 8 hours or overnight for flavors to blend.

Yield: 15 or more servings

Note: This is a dream come true for chocolate lovers. This decadent dessert has it all; easy preparation, beautiful, and so delicious.

Microwave Peanut Brittle

1	cup sugar		1	cup roasted, salted peanuts
½	cup light corn syrup		1	teaspoon vanilla extract
1	teaspoon margarine		¾	teaspoon baking soda

In a 2 quart glass bowl, blend sugar and corn syrup. Microwave on high power 6 to 8 minutes or until syrup turns a light brown color. Stir in margarine, peanuts, and vanilla extract; mix well. Microwave on high power 1 to 1½ minutes. Gently stir in baking soda until light and foamy. Pour mixture onto a large baking sheet that has been heavily greased with margarine. With spatula, lift edges of candy as it cools, pull until thin. When brittle is completely cool, break into small pieces. Store in airtight container.

Yield: 1 pound candy

Krazy Crunch Caramel Corn

2	quarts popped corn	2	sticks margarine
1⅓	cups pecans	½	cup light corn syrup
⅔	cup almonds	1	teaspoon vanilla extract
1⅓	cups sugar		

Combine popped corn, pecans, and almonds in a large bowl; stir to distribute ingredients; set aside. In a large saucepan, combine sugar, margarine, and corn syrup. Bring mixture to a boil, reduce heat and cook, stirring constantly until mixture turns a light caramel color. Stir in vanilla extract. Pour mixture over corn and nuts. Spread on a large baking sheet that has been greased with margarine. Cool; break into pieces. Store in airtight container.

Yield: 3 quarts

Pauline's Buttermilk Pralines

3	cups sugar	2	tablespoons white corn syrup
	Dash salt	2	sticks butter
1	teaspoon baking soda	1	teaspoon vanilla extract
1	cup buttermilk	1½	cups coarsely chopped pecans

In a heavy 5 quart Dutch oven, combine the sugar and the next 5 ingredients. Cook, stirring occasionally, over medium heat until candy thermometer registers hard-ball stage. A cup of ice water can also be used to test if it's at hard-ball stage. Remove from heat; add vanilla extract and pecans; set mixture aside to cool. When praline mixture begins to harden, beat until the color begins to get lighter. Spoon onto wax paper in patties. If first praline is too runny, beat mixture longer. Cool pralines and wrap in plastic wrap. Store in airtight container up to 3 weeks.

Yield: 3 dozen pralines

Note: Pralines and Mexican food are Texas traditions. This outstanding recipe was provided by a friend. She makes hundreds of these pralines each year for a fund raiser at her church.

Fresh Orange Sherbet

4	oranges	1	pint heavy cream
2	lemons	1	teaspoon vanilla extract
4	cups sugar		Milk to fill 1 gallon freezer

Squeeze juice from oranges and lemons. In a large bowl combine juice and sugar; stir until sugar is dissolved. Stir in heavy cream and vanilla. Pour mixture into a 1 gallon ice cream freezer; add enough milk to fill freezer. Chill in refrigerator. Freeze sherbet according to manufactures directions.

Yield: 1 gallon sherbet

Old-Fashioned
Vanilla Custard Ice Cream

5	cups milk	½	teaspoon salt
2¼	cups sugar	6	eggs, beaten
6	tablespoons all-purpose flour	4	cups heavy cream
		4½	teaspoons vanilla extract

In a medium saucepan, scald the milk; set aside. Combine sugar, flour, and salt in a 4 quart saucepan. Stir a small amount of the hot milk into the sugar mixture; blend. Slowly add the remaining hot milk; blend thoroughly. Cook mixture over low heat for about 10 minutes, stirring constantly until mixture is thickened. In a medium bowl, beat the eggs; add a small amount of the thickened custard to the eggs; whisk to blend. Slowly stir egg mixture into the custard mixture; cook mixture 1 minute longer. Cool mixture slightly and refrigerate until completely chilled. Pour custard mixture into a 1 gallon freezer; stir in cream and vanilla extract. Freeze mixture according to manufactures directions.

Yield: 1 gallon ice cream

Note: One of our wedding gifts was a hand crank ice cream freezer. This recipe and several others was included with it. The custard takes a little time to cook, but it's worth the effort.

Index

Index

Index

Index

Index

Index

Index

Index

Bobbie R. Adams
1911 Spring Hollow Path
Round Rock, Texas 78681-4052

Please send _____ copy(ies)   @ $19.95 each _____

Postage and handling   @ $ 3.50 each _____

Texas residents add sales tax   @ $ 1.65 each _____

Total _____

Name _____

Address _____

City _____ State _____ Zip _____

Make checks payable to *Bobbie R. Adams*

Bobbie R. Adams
1911 Spring Hollow Path
Round Rock, Texas 78681-4052

Please send _____ copy(ies)   @ $19.95 each _____

Postage and handling   @ $ 3.50 each _____

Texas residents add sales tax   @ $ 1.65 each _____

Total _____

Name _____

Address _____

City _____ State _____ Zip _____

Make checks payable to *Bobbie R. Adams*

Bobbie R. Adams
1911 Spring Hollow Path
Round Rock, Texas 78681-4052

Please send _____ copy(ies)   @ $19.95 each _____

Postage and handling   @ $ 3.50 each _____

Texas residents add sales tax   @ $ 1.65 each _____

Total _____

Name _____

Address _____

City _____ State _____ Zip _____

Make checks payable to *Bobbie R. Adams*